The Boss of You

THE
BOSS
of
YOU

*Everything a Woman
Needs to Know to Start,
Run, and Maintain
Her Own Business*

LAUREN BACON & EMIRA MEARS

SEAL PRESS

The Boss of You

Everything A Woman Needs to Know to Start, Run, and Maintain Her Own Business

Copyright © 2008 by Lauren Bacon and Emira Mears

Published by
Seal Press
A Member of the Perseus Books Group
1700 Fourth Street
Berkeley, California 94710

Library of Congress Cataloging-in-Publication Data

Mears, Emira.
  The boss of you : everything a woman needs to know to start, run, and maintain her own business by Emira Mears & Lauren Bacon.
     p. cm.
  Includes bibliographical references.
  ISBN-13: 978-1-58005-236-8
  ISBN-10: 1-58005-236-3
  1. New business enterprises—Management. 2. Women-owned business enterprises—Management. I. Bacon, Lauren. II. Title. III. Title: Everything a woman needs to know to start, run, and maintain her own business.

HD62.5.M42 2008
658.0082--dc22

                            2007039417

10 9 8 7 6 5

Cover design by Domini Dragoone
Interior design by Megan Cooney
Printed in the United States of America
Distributed by Publishers Group West

For every woman running a small business who is defining success on her own terms, bringing her values to work, and creating community along the way: We hope we've done you justice. And for those of you fantasizing about making your business dreams a reality: Welcome.

THE TABLE *of* CONTENTS

INTRODUCTION

So: You want to be the boss of you, right? We're guessing that's why you picked up this book. You've got an idea or a hobby that you absolutely love (or a skill you want to liberate from cubicle tyranny), and you're pretty darn sure that with the right plan in place you could launch your own creative, independent venture; pay the bills; and maybe even make more than you're making now. Whether your dream is to open the tastiest vegan bistro in town, to make and sell your one-of-a-kind hand-screened tea cozies online, or to start an all-female graphic design consultancy, your head is probably swimming with questions. Of course you're an expert at baking vegan lasagna/ sewing a tea cozy/designing a brochure, but what about all the details of business ownership? Do you need a business license? How will you do your taxes? Do you need a website? What about employees? And what's all this going to cost? These kinds of questions have probably cluttered up your head as you've pondered how to take the idea of doing what you love for a living from daydream to reality. We know all the questions you've got because we've been through it all, eight years and counting. As we took the path from "Hey, why don't we do this on our own?" to writing our first paycheck, we quickly learned that there was more to becoming your own boss than just figuring out what color your business cards should be.

At the time we set out on our entrepreneurial adventure, we scoured the bookstores for resources that would help answer our most basic questions about the details of business ownership and support us in figuring out what the big picture was really going to look like. Sure, there were plenty of books out there, but none of them spoke to us, or to the size and type of business we were looking to establish. Most seemed to assume that every businessperson was pushing for big growth, plenty of staff, and massive profits, and while we wouldn't have said no to a windfall, we knew that we wanted to start out small (just the two of us), work with people we loved, and grow at a sustainable rate over time while still being paid what we were worth. To be honest, it has always seemed to us that starting small and growing slowly was a much more reasonable—and achievable—approach than the high-stakes, adrenaline-filled business games that make financial headlines. Some people love living on the edge, but we're not among their number. We wanted to beat the odds and see our business survive a good long time—and we didn't want to have to work twenty-four hours a day to get there. We figured there had to be another path to entrepreneurship than the one we were seeing modeled in books and the media.

After thumbing through many dull business tomes (and frilly pastel books for "girl" entrepreneurs), we were able to put our finger on what it was about the other business books that didn't work for us: They wanted to tell us what success looked like. As fiercely independent and strong-willed gals, we were having none of it. So that's what makes this book different: We don't assume we know what success looks like for you, though we are going to help you figure out your own vision. Because the true beauty of being an entrepreneur is that you get to answer that question for yourself. (Then you get to work your butt off to make sure you achieve your dream.)

We've been inspired over the years by the many, many businesswomen we've met who are doing business in nontraditional ways, starting with setting their own standards for success. For some, success means earning a living wage while funneling a portion of their revenues to charities; for others, it means having a work schedule flexible enough that they can walk their kids to and from school every day; still others define success by being able to create a fantastic work environment for their staff. You'll have your own definition, and it may look quite different from these examples. We're here to tell you that you don't need to follow the herd to have a thriving business that sustains you for years to come. Just because your dreams don't include being described as a "tycoon" doesn't mean you can't experience life as a wildly successful entrepreneur!

This book is the savvy and oh-so-practical resource we wish we'd had in our early days. By the time you're finished reading it, if we've done our job, you'll have a clear sense of what's involved in running a business *your* way. We'll guide you through the process of defining what success looks like for you so that you can create a business that reflects your values, that's ethically sound, that serves your community, *and* that pays you (and your staff, if you choose to have any) what you're worth. And we'll help you work through the details of starting, running, and maintaining your soon-to-be-successful venture.

We've structured the book to follow all the stages your business will go through, from those initial brainstorming sessions to the first few years of running your own show. We'll start by helping you define what it is you're going to sell, who's going to buy it, and what it's all going to cost you. We'll help you decide what you're going to call yourself, and what kind of digs your new venture will require. Next, we'll move on to helping you figure out how you're going to let the world know that you and your new business exist (a.k.a. marketing). Marketing is just as important in the early days of your business as it is two years later when you decide you'd like to get a bit of a pay raise and so need to round up some more work. As any business owner can tell you, marketing is a story that never really ends, so the whole sec-tion is one you'll want to come back to over time (and that may hold some useful gems for those of you already a few years into being the boss of you). The last section in the book explores ways to grow and maintain your business over time. While much of that information is useful to consider in the early years—a girl's got to dream big, after all—a lot of it will become more relevant as time goes on. So if you're picking this book up after being your own boss for a few years, there's also wisdom here to help you navigate the challenges of your business as time passes.

But don't just take our word for it. In addition to sharing our own experiences, we've included examples and advice from some of the smartest businesswomen we could find, all of whom are running businesses like the one you want to create: the kind that jibes with the owner's values and personal goals. We've used their stories and fabulous wisdom throughout the book to illustrate the challenges and opportunities that being your own boss will bring.

One of the things that bothers us most about the way business is discussed out there in the world is how little time or space is given to profiling smaller, sustainable, and creative businesses. While we'd re-ally like to think that has nothing to do with how many of them are started by women, chances are that plays into it. It is our hope that the collected wisdom of the women we spoke to and the stories we tell in this book will help you realize that you aren't alone on this awesome journey to becoming your own boss. And, with any luck, this book will be one of the tools that help you on the way to becoming one of those examples that other women can learn from.

GETTING STARTED

GETTING STARTED
Introduction

WE'VE ALREADY ESTABLISHED that you want to start a business, and are reading this book either to guide you in taking those steps or to explore whether or not it's a viable option for you. Well, get out your pencil and put on your thinking cap—we've got work to do.

A lot of traditional business wisdom will tell you that you absolutely *must* write a formal business plan before you get started. While we're not ones to suggest skimping on doing all your homework, unless you're seeking outside investment or a bank loan, writing a formal business plan may not be the best way for you to spend your time. That said, there are a lot of components of a business plan that you need to spend some serious time thinking about before you quit your job or invest your life savings in bath bomb ingredients. And, as you may have already guessed, we're going to help you along your way.

The following four chapters cover a lot of ground, from initial plans and schemes right down to the ins and outs of pricing and finding the right name for your company. Believe it or not, this handful of chapters takes you right through from "I've got a dream" to your opening day. (So why are there two more sections? 'Cause just getting your doors open is not going to ensure that the rent gets paid and business sails along smoothly, silly.)

We're going to start with the fundamentals as we see them: First, you're going to set some business goals. Next, you'll define what success looks like for you, personally. We believe that in order to feel successful, you need to know what success means to you. After all, if you don't know what it looks like, how are you going to recognize it when it's staring you in the face? Then you'll figure out where your personal strengths lie, so you can make sure to get the help you need along the way.

Once you've set some goals, we'll go about making them a little more concrete. You'll define what you're going to be selling, and who you'll be selling to—the core elements of every business. Those may seem like questions with obvious answers, but in fact, it takes quite a bit of effort to answer them well. (Here's a hint: "Everyone" is *not* your target market.)

And of course, we'll talk in depth about money—how much you'll need to get started, how to create a budget, and how to price your wares. You may or may not consider money to be your friend, but better your friend than your enemy, right? Plus, it turns out you can do a whole lot with it. And really, we'd love for you to have plenty of it.

The last chapter in this section will guide you through the various steps in bringing your business to life: coming up with the perfect name, finding the right location (even if it's that sunny corner of your bedroom), and getting your legal and financial ducks in a row. By the time you reach the end, you should be well on your way to hanging out your shingle.

If you're as eager to get to that last step as we were when we started out, you've possibly skipped ahead to the good stuff already. For the rest of you, let's get on with it.

CHAPTER 1

Define Your Vision

WHAT MADE YOU PICK up this book? Do you already have a crystal-clear vision of the business you want to create? Or is it a bit fuzzy around the edges? Even if you're still in the idle curiosity stage, there is one thought that must have entered your mind at some point or other:

What if I could do my own thing, be my own boss, and make a living at it?

Well, before we get into all the glorious details of how you can do that, we want to make sure you've got a solid handle on *why* you want to do it. That way, when you get into the trickier decisions that will follow, you'll have something to come back to—a set of goals for your business that makes sense for you.

So, sharpen your pencils: Welcome to the Chapter of Great Big Lists!

One of the things that make our partnership such a great one is our differences. While we are regularly known to finish each other's sentences in public, and on more than one occasion have shown up at a function in verging-on-matching outfits, we are in fact

> *not exactly the same person. When we first started the company, Lauren was passionate about reading every book she could lay her hands on that looked like it could be of use to us. She is the reigning queen of going through exercises and lists to get focused on the challenges ahead. Emira, on the other hand, tends to work through one list and then decide she's probably nailed all there is to know— and begins to get a bit itchy about getting started. But it didn't take long before Emira came around to Lauren's approach—and while we can hear you squirming in your chair (and flipping ahead to the next chapter) from here, we urge you to stick around. The time for moving ahead at full tilt is coming soon, we promise.*

❁ Bringing Home the Bacon *(Vegan Options Available)*

When Lauren was an impressionable first-year university student, she decided it would be a great idea to sign up for Economics 101. (This was all part of her grand scheme to infiltrate the hallways of power and take over the world. Alas, Econ 101 pretty much wiped out that plan.) On the first day of classes, the teacher got up in front of the hundreds of students crowding the lecture hall and announced the founding principle of the entire year's curriculum: "Businesses exist for one reason: to make money." At that moment, Lauren should have walked right out of there and enrolled in a nice Feminist Film course. But she didn't, and found herself totally baffled. Was this guy telling her that she would never be a successful businessperson because she thought there was more behind it than a grab for cash?

Whenever we find ourselves checking out the business section of the newspaper or bookstore, we get the same feeling of mild confusion. Most of the discourse about the world of business is totally focused on making money. End of story. And while in the end, money is certainly a factor for our own business—if we didn't make any, it would be a hobby, not a day job—it wasn't the only thing on our list of goals when we started out.

Each business is a reflection of its owners, and we suspect that's even more the case for those of you reading this book—because if you were the sort of person who only cared about making the most money in the shortest possible time frame, you probably would have picked up one of those other "how to succeed" business books that have a cover photo of a dude on a yacht. Chances are, you've got a host of reasons why you want to start your own business, and here's where you get to write them all down.

▶ When we started our business we were pretty clear on why we wanted to do it. We had been daydreaming about it over soy lattes and cocktails for months: wanting to be the ones calling the shots, no longer working for someone else's dream, making more money, working with the clients we wanted to work with, and so on. But that list was really more about the things we didn't like about our current jobs. What about the things we hadn't yet allowed ourselves to dream about, like working in an office space where we could see the ocean every day, setting a budget for professional development, and having a chance to meet some of our idols and mentors in the field as colleagues? It's worth taking the time to imagine what your job might bring you in your wildest, most successful dreams.

While we can't guarantee that every fantasy on your list will come true—the ones involving private jets are particularly tricky—it's a fact that you're more likely to realize your ideas if you've taken the time to think them through and write them down. And conversely, if you don't give yourself a chance to dream a little, you'll be stuck within the limits of your stale old ideas, from modest paychecks to overlong work hours. When you're at the helm of your business, you'll be responsible for producing all of your own rewards, so if you ever want to surprise yourself with your own successes, you'd better ask yourself what secret desires you've been keeping cocooned within. Once you give yourself a chance to set some goals that really inspire you, you'll be amazed at how they start to "magically" materialize. (The "magic," of course, is the power of intention.)

❀ Exercise #1: Business Goals

To get you started, here are some of the answers we've heard from other established and aspiring businesswomen we know:

- To spend my days doing my own thing (e.g., designing clothes, teaching yoga, managing PR for innovative businesses, selling the best in quality sex toys to couples who care), rather than sitting at a desk answering phones.

- To be able to work less (or with more-flexible hours) than I do now, so that I can spend more time with my kid(s)/family, pursuing my hobby as an amateur cross-country unicyclist, or perfecting my ollie.

- To have the opportunity to travel to faraway places and see the world as a legitimate part of my job—or simply to have more time off to travel.

- To make enough money to buy a house, expand my shoe collection, spend part of the year as a surf diva, or _____.

- To work with the clients I love, not the ones my boss puts on my desk.

- To ensure that I always get to have final say.

- To support my personal cause, _____ (e.g., creating environmentally friendly menstrual products, making clothes for women of any size so we can all feel like fashionistas, supporting animal rights through cruelty-free body products, etc.).

- To get paid to explore my creative side rather than feeling like I have to leave it to my spare time.

· To serve an underserved client base/market that is absolutely pining to get its hands on what I have to offer.

Here's some space for your list—get busy:

> To have time to travel,
> stay healthy (gym, running,
> soccer/hockey, yoga) and
> volenteer while still having
> enough money to pay for it

Now, hang on to this list; we'll be coming back to it.

❊ *I Want It All!*

If your list is a long one—or if, upon looking it over, you wonder if it's really possible to achieve all of your goals—you may want to prioritize it. You can either list your goals in descending order of importance, or break the list into "must-haves," "nice-to-haves," and "maybe someday when all my dreams come true"—whatever seems to fit you best. Ultimately, it's important that you not try to accomplish every one of your life goals through your business; don't forget that you still need ways to have fun on weekends, and sadly it may not be practical to build your business around your stilt-walking hobby.

❊ Defining Success

Here's a quick exercise to determine whether your list of business goals is complete: If you were to achieve everything on your list, would you consider yourself a raging success? If the answer is no, try going back and refining it further. But if you're feeling like you're off to a pretty good start, we'll move on to the next step: setting some parameters for success.

When you are the one running the ship every day it can be hard sometimes to remember where you are going or even to notice when you get there. Once your business gets going, there are so many things to do and details to focus on that it is really easy to lose sight of what you wanted in the first place. That's why you need to have a clear idea of how you will define success.

THE UNTOLD STORIES OF SUCCESS

One of the things that compelled us to write this book was the lack of business books that tell you it's okay not to want to strike it rich. Now of course, if untold riches managed to find their way to us, it's not like we wouldn't invite them in for tea, but that's not what we had in mind when we set out to start a business. Financially speaking, our goals were pretty simple: to start and maintain a business that would pay us the salary we felt we were worth, including an excellent extended health plan. Starting an IT company in the late 1990s meant that most people assumed we were hedging our bets on an IPO or some big cash injection, and we spent the first few years constantly defending our modest business model. This is not to say that striking it rich is a bad goal—just that it may not be your number one driving force. So, if making enough to pay the bills and take four weeks' vacation a year is enough for you, right on. Don't second-guess what you really want out of life just because it doesn't fit with what you think you should want.

Take a moment to look ahead . . . down the path a ways, when you've been in business a while and can reflect back on your achievements. What are the things that will make you proudest? Will it be the day your favorite local celebrity stopped by your store and gushed at length about how great your pants make her butt look? Or is it going to be the month you managed to surpass your old salary? Maybe the idea of being home to send your daughter off to school, and greet her when she gets home, is the ultimate reward. Whatever it is that gets your juices flowing, set it down on paper right this instant! These are the visions that will keep you going during the more challenging days of self-employment.

Hint: Try to be as specific as possible. The more concrete you can be, the more likely you'll be to reach your goals.

❀ *Exercise #2: Personal Measures of Success*

Sample answers—I will know I'm successful when:

- I make more money than I do now.

- I am working no more than ___ hours a week.

- I see myself or my work on the front cover of a magazine/paper.

- I land an invitation to speak at a conference.

- I can afford to put a down payment on a drum kit/house/ piece of art.

- I find myself looking forward to Monday morning.

- I have a roster of clients that I love working with.

Okay, your turn!

- Having a flexible schedule
- feel my work is valued

I DON'T WANNA WRITE ANYTHING DOWN!

Are any of these thoughts going through your head?

I'll do this later . . . Looks suspiciously like work to me! . . . What if I change my mind later? . . . I bet if I sleep on it, I'll come up with something better tomorrow . . . I don't have a pen handy . . .

Stop! Get up, grab the nearest pencil, and jot down a few thoughts. They don't have to be brilliant, or final, or anything—but you need to do it now. Why? Because it really, truly makes a difference to be able to look back on these goals later and see whether they still hold true, whether they need adjusting, and how far you've come. You'll honestly be amazed at how helpful this stuff is when you're looking back a year from now and want to get a handle on how you're doing. Otherwise, you'll end up holding yourself to unspoken standards—like an unconscious belief that until you're lunching with power brokers every day, you haven't made it—which are almost always impossible to live up to!

❀ *Do What You Do Best (and Farm Out the Rest)*

You now have a set of business goals, as well as your personal measures of success. The final piece of your visioning puzzle has to do with identifying your core skills. This exercise will help you evaluate where to focus your energies, and where to ask for help. Knowing all of this will be particularly important when your business really gets going and you find yourself wishing there were extra hours in the day.

What are your strongest assets? Unless you're opening a restaurant here, your killer pumpkin cheesecake doesn't count; we're talking about business skills. Things like your ability to multitask—very handy for administrivia and the daily running of almost any business. Or maybe it's your fearlessness when it comes to meeting new people, which will make you great at getting new business or selling your products. When you are making this list, don't just think of it as a list of qualities that you might include on a standard job application, or skills that you know you've learned in "the workplace." If you're thinking about becoming an entrepreneur, chances are you've got a lot of extra-curricular stuff going on that you can draw from as well. Skills you've picked up organizing the monthly drag cabaret, volunteering at the farmers market, and keeping all the girls getting along at intramural soccer are valuable talents that are going to be very helpful in your new venture. Many women find it's in their spare-time pursuits that they developed their most critical business skills—whether it's because they've been stuck in a thankless job with little room for upward mobility, or taken time out of the rat race to have kids . . . or have always known that their expertise has long gone untapped at their day job.

Now: What things do you absolutely dread? Are there things you know you'll keep ignoring until one day they pile up so high they need their own zip code? Or maybe there are skills that you know aren't your strong suit, and you're okay with that. For us, it's taxes. That's not to say we don't file them—because we've seen others make that mistake and it's not a pretty picture! But we don't want to be the ones to keep on top of the seemingly random and wildly complex rules of income tax, so every year we take our file of sorted receipts down to our favorite bookkeeper's office and she makes it all better for us. Easy as pie. And it's well worth the few hours of her time we pay for; we're just *so* much happier not worrying about it.

It's helpful to know these things from the start, but it becomes invaluable as your business gets busier; a clear list of your competencies and less-than-favorite tasks will help you to reflect carefully on what you're willing to delegate, and what you'd rather keep a close eye on. And it will help to remind you what it is that you love to do at work.

> ► Tiffany Threadgould of RePlayGround makes eco-gifts out of recycled materials. It's creative work, but it also requires a lot of attention to detail on the product design and manufacturing side of things. Tiffany's currently running things solo, but she found an intern to help her out with the hands-on stuff so that she can focus on what she does best: coming up with new ideas, marketing her wares, and running the business. Her eventual goal is to offload the manufacturing entirely to someone else. When you're clear on your strengths, delegating gets a whole lot easier—even for do-it-yourself types—and that's crucial if you want to deliver the highest-quality goods and stay focused and efficient.

Don't be surprised if this is one of the most challenging exercises for you; often it's difficult for us to identify our own strongest and weakest qualities, and even if we know ourselves really well, it can be tough to put it down on paper. In our experience, it tends to be harder for women to speak up about our accomplishments than it is for many men—so try to put yourself in an expansive, generous frame of mind, and get ready to blow yourself away! Imagine you're your own mentor, and are offering up words of wisdom; you might be surprised to hear what your "teacher self" has to say about those hours of patient homework help you offered your neighbor's kid (excellent communication skills and creative brainstorming ability!) or your vast network of friends and acquaintances (born marketer!).

And remember, just as it can be handy to get your best gal pal to write your bio for that web personals ad you're thinking of placing, friends can be a great resource when you're going through this exercise. You may want to grab a couple of friends or a family member for a coffee (buttering them up with homemade banana bread isn't cheating!) and have them list out some of your best qualities and—if you're brave—weak points. Be sure to write down everything they give you, but don't feel like you have to take it all as gospel truth. If your sister insists you're no good with money because she never got over the time you raided her piggy bank, let it go and move on to the stuff about how your years of working at summer camp make you a great team leader, and make a note that you've got skills in management and conflict resolution.

Finally, don't get too stuck on what you've done in the past. If you've never done any marketing per se, but you're confident you're the best person to handle those aspects of your business, write it down anyway. If you change your mind later, you can always bring in some help—but what we're looking for here is a set of guidelines to help you get focused as you're getting started.

When you've had a chance to work through your initial list, as well as the contributions of your lovely assistants, try to get concrete about how your personal qualities can contribute to your business. In our example below, we've assembled a list of what our sample business gal might want to focus on in her aromatherapy company, along with some of the stuff she might want a hand with.

❊ Exercise #3: Skills, Strengths, and Passions

Sample: Aromatherapy Company

What I do best is
- product design: coming up with creative new formulas;
- quality control: keeping an eye on the details;
- customer service/sales;
- visioning: developing and refining a vision for the company that will inspire others.

It's not my strong suit, but I absolutely love
- marketing.

Although it makes me nervous, I will learn to deal with
- money: bookkeeping, developing financial scenarios such as cash flow projections, finding investors.

I would rather walk across hot coals than
- deal with the press.

If I had to, I could give up or share
- day-to-day operations: managing production facilities, answering phones and email.

Once you've got your own Skills, Strengths, and Passions list together, pair it with your Business Goals and Personal Measures of Success. This is your "holy trinity" of visioning documents; put them in a folder (ours is a bright, colorful one with stickers on it) and set it down somewhere you can refer to it often. Or, if you know that putting it in a folder means you're likely to never look at it again, then get all *Teen Beat* on yourself and tack it to the wall. Our friend Signy is a big fan of making things a bit more concrete than just a list on paper. When she wants something to stick in her mind she gets out a stack of magazines, some glitter, and her trusty glue stick—and creates a glossy collage that quite literally makes her goals sparkle. Then she hangs it up beside her desk, on the fridge, or above the phone, where she's sure to see it all the time. Do whatever works for you to make all these ideas feel real (though getting a "measures of success" tattoo might be a bit pricey).

❀ *Girls (and Boys) on the Side:*
A Word on Business Partnerships

Let's take a little detour into the world of partnerships. You may have already set your heart on sharing the reins with someone else, or you might notice that your Skills, Strengths, and Passions list has a particularly large gap in it that might be best filled by a partner rather than an employee or subcontractor. Whether or not to go into business with a partner is one of the most significant decisions you can make. Some of the factors that will play into this decision are:

Complementary skill sets: Many business partnerships are born of necessity; one partner has the technical know-how, while the other is a natural salesperson . . . and so on;

Financial concerns: Businesses that require a significant investment of start-up money may tap a pool of investing partners, each of whom has a stake in the business;

Friends and relations: It's quite common for friends and family members to go into business together; the existing relationship can form a strong base for the various challenges of running a business, and ensures that when things get rough, you have someone to talk to who really gets what you're going through.

If you do decide to go into business with a partner (and we must say, from our personal experience, it's a great way to go!), you absolutely must do one thing:

Sign a Partnership Agreement

This has a tendency to be one of those things that people procrastinate on, like writing thank-you cards or cleaning under the fridge. We cannot stress enough how important it is to get an agreement drawn up, reviewed by a lawyer, and signed . . . as soon as possible in the life of your business. This is the document that outlines what will happen in all of those scenarios you can hardly imagine right now . . . like when one of you decides to leave the business, or when one of you becomes unable to work, or any number of other possibilities that could cause you untold grief if you don't have a plan in writing.

Here's why it's important. Imagine this scenario (based on a true story):

Three friends start a company together, as partners. As time goes on, they develop a roster of clients, hire employees, and move into a big, beautiful office space. Eventually, Partner A decides it's time to move on. There's no partnership agreement, so the three partners sit down to negotiate what should happen next: Will the two remaining partners buy Partner A out? Will A get some kind of "severance package"? How does ownership get divided for Partners B and C?

Well, as luck would have it, Partner A's sister is a lawyer, who steps in and informs B and C that because there's no partnership agreement, they can either accept A's offer or get themselves into a long and costly legal battle. The remaining partners don't have a leg to stand on (and they can't afford to go to court), so they end up paying off Partner A in spades, and in the process, their friendships with A are irreversibly damaged—not to mention the sleepless nights and emotional torment they went through during the confrontational and ultimately unfair negotiation process.

Please, we beg of you: Get it in writing, and do it now. The time will come when you'll need it—and you'll be glad you took care of it early on.

❀ *Well, How Fabulous Are You?*

Congratulations on completing the first steps on your entrepreneurial journey! We hope you're starting to feel a little clearer about what you want out of your business—and a bit more confident about your ability to do it. (If you're still nervous, just remember: Women-run businesses have a much higher success rate than the ones with men at the helm—so you've already got the odds stacked in your favor!)

Treat yourself to a reward (an outing, a copy of your favorite magazine, a pastry, or whatever tickles your fancy) before you tackle the next chapter: You've earned it!

CHAPTER 2
Have a Plan

NOW THAT WE HAVE CONVINCED you that you, too, can be the mistress of your own domain (we *have* convinced you, haven't we?), it's time to make your vision a reality. Starting with the goals that you outlined in the last section, you will now need to start connecting the dots so you'll have a clearer picture of where you're headed.

If you have your lists from Chapter 1 (your Business Goals; Personal Measures of Success; and Skills, Strengths, and Passions), you've got all the tools you need. The next step is to answer three questions:

1. What are you selling?

2. Who are your customers?

3. Do you want or expect the answers to questions 1 and 2 to change in the first two years of your business?

If you think those first two things are no-brainers, hang tight for a few more pages—you may find that they aren't as simple as they look. "What you're selling" may seem simple if you're making felt accessories—but consider for a moment that you may also be selling a feeling (like comfort), or an idea (such as artisanship), along with the products themselves.

And if your immediate answer to item 2 is "everyone," then boy howdy, do you need to read this chapter!

▶ In one of the many business books we've read over the years, we came across a great example of the "What am I selling?" conundrum. A years-old company selling wheelchairs, walkers, and other equipment for people with disabilities was having some growth challenges, and they decided they needed a fresh perspective on what it was, exactly, that they were really selling. Their answer? Freedom. Once they'd shifted their perspective from selling tools to selling an idea, they were able to open their minds and figure out how to better serve their customers.

By the end of this chapter, you should not only be on solid ground with respect to your business goals but you should also start to see how your business is going to look through other people's eyes—from your customers, to your bank (should you require a start-up loan), to prospective partners and staff. This is an important step, as it will help you shift your focus from what *you* want out of the company to what your customers want—which is kind of helpful if you want to be able to, you know, *sell* stuff to them.

❋ Big Question #1: What's for Sale?

So how do you figure out what it is you're actually selling? This will, of course, vary according to the type of business you're setting up. If you're designing furniture, that's a pretty concrete start to your answer right there. On the other hand, if you've been tackling research projects on a freelance basis and have decided to set up a consultancy, that's another matter entirely. Either way, though, you're going to want to figure out how to explain to other people what it is you do—and how to explain it with some flair, so that you don't get lost in the crowd.

Here are some questions to get you started (those lists from Chapter 1 may come in handy here):

What's the core of my business? At the end of the day, you should be able to sum up your business in a single sentence. It may not encompass the full breadth of your work, but it should get the key elements across. For now, we're looking for the baseline description—the one you'd use to fill in a form, or explain to your second cousin what you do for a living. (In other words, this ain't the place for the "freedom" bit we discussed above.) So you might be selling fridge magnets, or massage therapy, or graphic design work. . . . This might seem like a silly question, but if you aren't clear on this part, you'll only get more confused from here on in. (One final piece of advice here: Try to be as detailed as possible—e.g., "portrait photography services" or "local and organically grown plants and gardening supplies," rather than "photography" or "garden stuff." For example, Teri Dimalanta, who runs Giddy Giddy, describes her line of hair accessories as "handcrafted felt hair clips for babies and little girls.")

How will I deliver the goods? Sometimes what sets you apart isn't just *what* you're selling, it's *how* you sell it. Products might be sold wholesale, retail, or both; at craft fairs, over the Internet, or in your own storefront; service providers might plan on working primarily as subcontractors, or directly with clients. Or perhaps you're setting up a consultancy. What services are you planning to offer? Will you be working alone, or do you plan to hire staff (or take on partners) at some point? Are you focusing on a particular subject area, or do you want to keep things varied? Do you plan on working at your client's offices, or mainly from your home?

What motivates me to do what I'm doing? Sometimes, although the product is easy to describe (like those fridge magnets), there's something else going on behind the scenes that's a bit more theoretical— but that cuts to the heart of your business. Maybe the fridge magnets came about as a way for you to design creative home accessories to brighten up people's lives and provide a sustainable income for the stay-at-home moms who help with your production. Experiment with a few answers, and hang on to all the ones that feel strong to you . . . they'll come in handy a bit later on.

Cinnamon Cooper started Poise bags as a way to increase the amount of money she donated to her favorite charities. She knew that her own income limited how much she could donate, but that if she started a successful business that donated a percentage of its sales, her ability to support the causes that mattered to her would increase.

What's my scope? Are you going global, staying local, or something in between? Do you plan on working on small-scale or large projects? Will you be expanding your product line over time? How many clients do you intend to juggle at one time? Try to get a sense of how broad your range of work is. (And there's no right answer here—sometimes small is beautiful.) In five years, when your business is wildly successful, your products and services may need to change. You can always revise your business plan down the road; for now, set yourself a range that feels achievable (while still stretching you a little—challenging yourself is good!).

For example, when we started Raised Eyebrow, we thought we'd be working primarily with women small business owners in and around Vancouver, as well as nonprofit groups. That seemed like our ideal market at the time, because those two groups were where most of our personal contacts lay. Seven years later, though, our client base has expanded to include national and international clients, larger nonprofits, and some bigger businesses as well. However, we've stuck with our original goal to specialize exclusively in website design and development—it's what we do best, and we don't want to spread ourselves too thin.

What kind of personality does my business have? Try to get a handle on how you want your business to be perceived by your customers. If you're making belt buckles, are they arty, DIY, or classic (or all three)?

Are you a tailored-suit kind of organization, or a let-your-hair-down organic food co-op? We'll delve into this more a little later on, but for now, some broad brushstrokes will do.

Where do I fit in? You should have some idea of what the competition is up to, and how your business compares. Are you the high-end, top-notch tattoo shop? The health-conscious, organic deli? Or perhaps you're planning on using your years of nonprofit volunteer work to your advantage in your new career as a communications consultant? List the things that set you apart from the other kids on the block. (By the way, marketers call this "positioning," so if you want to come off as a pro, drop that term into your conversations and watch people nod sagely.)

Are you starting to feel like you have a handle on what it is you're selling? Hopefully you've been able to do some fine-tuning on your business idea, taking it from "research and consulting services" to something like "research and consulting services in the field of health and wellness, performed by a small and flexible team of expert contractors." Now that the Big Question has been answered, the rest should fall into place fairly easily.

> *Depending on the nature of your business, one of these questions may turn out to be more interesting than the others—if so, make a note of that. It may be that your product or service (question 1) is so unique that it sets you apart. On the other hand, it may be that personality (question 5) is going to be the key to your success as an approachable, no-bull legal firm. Most likely it will be a combination of the various elements that produces your recipe for success, but often one or two will dominate.*

❧ A Visit to the Specialist

Many budding entrepreneurs are afraid of overspecializing, thinking that they're cutting off potential customers. While a size-9-only shoe store might be pushing it, don't shy away from defining your territory and sticking to it; many customers appreciate a clear-cut specialty, and some of the most successful businesses we know have a very distinct focus. Large businesses can afford to be "one-stop shops": think department stores, supermarkets, global ad agencies, or big law firms. But to really set your small business apart, specializing is the way to go. If you can do one thing very, very well, you'll become known as the "go-to" shop for your particular specialty, whether it's flavored olive oils you're selling or Thai massage.

You can specialize in any number of ways: by client base (such as a copywriter who works with arts groups), by product or service offerings (like Jenny Hart at Sublime Stitching, who sells incredibly funky embroidery patterns), or both (e.g., organic aromatherapy products for moms and babies).

The more precise you can be about your niche, the easier your sales become, because you're not trying to be all things to all people (an impossible job at the best of times!)—you can focus on the people who matter to you, and let the rest take a back seat.

So give your niche some thought. How can you set yourself apart from the competition? Will you offer lower prices? Better customer service? More specialized expertise? One-of-a-kind products? You'll want to have a very good idea of what your selling points are, because the more specialized you are, the easier it is for you to market yourself to the right people, sell your wares, and, most importantly, produce happy customers.

❧ *What's Your Type?*

This will probably not astonish you, but people really aren't that rational. (Thanks, Mr. Spock, for pointing that out.) When we make decisions about where to spend our money, we're almost as emotionally driven as we are in the romance department. If this weren't true, there would be no such thing as Chanel or Nike—no trends or outrageous splurging, just careful decisions based on comfort and affordability.

Now, there are people who spend their entire lives trying to get at the heart of what drives customer loyalty, but one major element is personality (also referred to by some as branding—we'll stick with personality, but they're interchangeable). Your business has its own personality, which may or may not be tied to your own. Betsey Johnson the clothing line and Betsey Johnson the person are likely pretty closely tied—but for most businesses, the owner(s) and the products and services are more distinct.

The trick is to make sure the outside (from your relationships with clients to your marketing) reflects the inside (your vision for the company), and the key to that is to get clear on what exactly your business personality *is*. Here's an exercise to help you get there.

❧ *Define Your Business's Personality*

One of our favorite exercises for developing a business personality is to imagine that business as a person (or other animate or inanimate object, if you prefer). If your business were to walk into the room, what would it be wearing? What foods, drinks, movies, magazines, and travel destinations would appeal? How would it interact with your customers?

Some people like to use celebrities (or fictional archetypes) as starting points for this exercise, so if that works for you, go for it. Just make sure you write down what aspects of that personality you're thinking about, so that you're clear about the fact it's Artemis's clear-headedness you're going for, not necessarily the "great huntress" bit.

We've listed a few questions to get you started:

If you were describing your business as a person, what character-istics would it have? Is it sophisticated or folksy? Laid-back or per-fectionist? Intellectual, sensual, competitive, serious, playful, artistic, approachable, funny, caring, chatty, grand, careful, calculating, impul-sive, reserved, outgoing, ambitious, socially conscious, cutting-edge, a dreamer, an aesthete? List as many qualities as you can think of, then narrow it down to your top five, and prioritize them.

What colors, tastes, and smells come to mind when you think of your business? Is it a vibrant, spicy red, or cool, clean white? Crisp, fragrant emerald green, like dill? Or a soft, worn-denim blue?

What kind of clothes would your business wear? Are we talking de-signer labels, coveralls, flannel pajamas?

Describe a meal that would reflect your business's personality. Is it a four-course fancy-pants affair? A simple, nutritious, family-style din-ner? Breakfast in bed with fresh-squeezed juice?

List three people (famous or not) who epitomize an aspect of your business, and explain what qualities they share with it. For example . . . Oprah Winfrey: ability to personally connect with others, sense of humor; Kathleen Hanna: independence, grassroots politics, creative drive, sass; my sister: all of the above, plus earthy, outdoorsy style and high energy.

Jot down any thoughts that come to mind. See if they begin to form into a coherent whole. You may want to take it a step further and develop an actual mascot (although we can't condone silly outfits for your pet). The main thing is to start to develop an idea of how you want other people to perceive your business, so you can project a con-sistent personality through everything you do. This will come in handy when you start looking at expanding, because you'll need to evaluate each potential new product and service to ensure it works with your company's existing personality—if not, either the new idea gets the boot, or you undertake a rebranding process.

❀ *Sizing Up the Competition*

One quick way to get a handle on what your business *is* is by determining what it *isn't*. Take a look around at your competition, and sniff out the bits you intend to do differently.

For most of us, our businesses are not unique—and whether or not we look at business as a popularity contest, our livelihoods depend on our being able to distinguish ourselves from the pack. (That doesn't mean you shouldn't partner with companies offering similar products and services, by the way—it just means you should be able to explain to your customers in ten words or fewer how you're different.)

As you're examining the marketplace and determining how you're going to fit in, there are two major issues to consider:

How you compare to the competition. Are you bigger, smaller, more expert? If you're smaller (and intend to stay that way), you can capitalize on the strengths inherent to smaller companies, such as agility, flexibility, and high-touch customer service. These qualities should come across in everything you do.

Your customers' motivations for buying your products and services. If you're making custom jewelry, your clients come to you for unique, handcrafted designs; you won't want to blend in with those accessory shops in the mall.

Your competitors will not only give you some ideas about how to position yourself to customers—they may also spark some thoughts about structuring your business, from store hours to relative pricing. It's not a great idea to lift ideas from your direct competitors, but you might want to go online and look around at similar businesses in other locations (or serving different niches) and see if you can't pick up a few tips (and thereby avoid reinventing the wheel). And don't limit yourself to businesses in your category; some of the best inspiration we got when starting out was from totally unrelated companies—primarily those we had interacted with as customers, friends, or colleagues.

Are you under the impression you don't have competitors? If you're the lone bakery in a ten-mile radius, you may be right—but that supermarket down the road may be selling baked goods, and you'd better have a good reason why your customers should make an extra stop on their shopping trips.

Finally, think about potential synchronicities with businesses that might not be competing with you directly. Are there other businesses around that target the same customers as yours, but that you wouldn't consider competition? (You might want to think about setting up shop nearby, if your business relies on foot traffic—or approaching the business owners with co-promotion ideas.)

❧ Big Question #2: Who Are Your Customers?

The next crucial piece of info you're going to need is who's going to buy whatever fabulous thing it is you're selling. There are many ways to break this down—your standard business books are going to call this "target market demographics" or some such thing, but basically what it boils down to is knowing your audience. Chances are that white males over the age of sixty living in the Midwest are not the primary market for your burlesque-style pasties and frilly-bottomed panties— so who is? You can break this down however it makes the most sense for your business; remember, the idea is to help make it easier for you to find these people so you can target your business toward them, so you want to get specific, and make a note of primary, secondary, and even tertiary markets.

If your potential customers consist primarily of *individuals*:	If your potential customers consist primarily of *organizations*:
• Do they belong to a particular gender, ethnicity, and/or age group? • What is their average income level? • Do they share a particular education level, occupation, or hobby? • What kinds of lives do they lead? Are they urban, cat-owning cyclists? (Make sure you've got a bike rack close at hand.) Nocturnal, coffee-drinking cool kids? (You might want to cater your hours of operation accordingly.)	• Are they from a particular sector or industry (e.g., nonprofits, local restaurants, clothing retailers, etc.)? • How big are they? Consider factors like number of employees, locations, and reach (local/national/international). • What is their average annual budget for your products/ services? • What are the characteristics of the key decision makers (i.e., the people you'll be closing the deal with)? Do they have a particular title? Do they have any common traits or needs? (For example, a lot of our clients are in the nonprofit sector, and they appreciate our experience working with large committees and boards.)

And here are a few more questions that apply to both types of customers:

Where are they located? This can be as specific as a particular neighborhood, or as broad as "North America and Europe," depending on your business.

How will they use your product or service? Are they likely to see you often, or just once in a while? What are the circumstances surrounding your interactions with them? (For example, a hair stylist might see her customers once every one to three months for an hour or two, booked casually on an as-needed basis.)

How much do they understand about your product or service? Are they novices or casual buyers, or experts who will go out of their way to find your little niche?

What are they looking to get out of buying what you're selling? This might go beyond the material product—for example, your homemade granola might attract customers looking for good health and good value, and who prefer to buy local and organic for environmental and political reasons.

❉ Your Mission (Should You Choose to Accept It)

Every old business book in the world wants you to write a mission statement—so why are we including it? Well, turns out those books aren't wrong about this particular bit. A mission statement, done well, can serve you excellently in terms of defining what your business is all about. (Done badly, of course, it can turn out like the yawn-worthy, jargon-laden stuff of sketchy megacorp wannabes . . . but you can likely avoid that fate by excluding the words "leverage," "maximize," and "interoperability.")

Your mission statement can be as creative as you like, although if you expect others are going to read it (such as lending institutions, or visitors to your website), you'll want to make sure it's clear and concise. But in general, this is your space to dream big, and write about the *purpose* of your business, beyond the day-to-day operations. The main components of a well-crafted mission statement are

big-picture goals: What, ultimately, do you hope to achieve through your business?

method: How will you get there?

values: What are the underlying principles that fuel your work?

Your mission can incorporate some of the answers you came up with in the previous exercise: Products, services, motivations and values, scope, personality, and positioning all have a place here. In fact, this is the perfect place to try to collect all of those bits and pieces and turn them into a unified whole.

There are no two ways about it: Creating a mission statement is a tough assignment. A lot of entrepreneurs start out knowing they have a vision, but have trouble putting it down in words. Feel free to go back to your lists from Chapter 1—your business goals and personal measures of success, in particular, should help you out. You may find you've got the raw materials there for a mission statement, once you liven them up a little. You know what you're selling—now, what's the big picture? If you're starting up a femme-friendly garage, your mission might begin, "We're the honest mechanics you tell your friends about."

Your mission statement doesn't need to be long; it can be as short as a single sentence, or you can write a paragraph or a bulleted list. If you need some inspiration, go online and search for the phrase "mission statement," followed by the name of a business you're interested in. That's what we did, and in the process we found some examples that inspired us (as well as some that didn't—and knowing what you *don't* want is helpful, too).

You want something that is both descriptive of what you do and visionary enough to motivate you in the future. (That said, you will probably revise it over the lifespan of your business; it doesn't need to last forever, so don't lose sleep in the quest for perfection.) Imagine that five years from now you're being presented with an award for your achievements in business—how would you like your work to be described, at its best and most inspirational level?

Don't be afraid to lighten things up with a little humor. One of our favorite mission statements—from Betsy Ross Patterns—is a fantastic combination of straight-talk and sass:

BETSY ROSS CONSTITUTION

We at Betsy Ross believe that it shouldn't be so darn hard to make hot clothes. We believe in good-looking clothes and flattering fits. We believe that all of the shoulder pads in the world should be piled up and lit on fire. We offer women the chance to make their clothes instead of buying them. Freedom!

Once you've got something you're happy with, get creative about how to use your mission statement. You may want to post it up on your wall, turn it into a screen saver . . . or go the more traditional route and work it into your marketing materials. The main thing is to make sure you regularly revisit your mission statement—it can be your guiding light in the months and years ahead, and the foundation you return to whenever you find yourself losing sight of your goals.

❀ *Target Practice*

We've saved our favorite exercise for last. We love this one so much we consider it to be play—not work at all. The goal is simple: to identify the types of people you want as your customers (a.k.a. your target market). And the best, and most fun, way of doing this that we know about is to develop profiles representing your key customer types.

To get the most out of this exercise, sit down and sketch out the broad categories of customers you're aiming for, and then tackle one category at a time. So if you expect your client base to consist of twenty-five- to forty-five-year-old urban hipsters, you might want to flesh out profiles for a twenty-six-year-old art school student, a game designer in his mid-thirties, and a forty-two-year-old novelist. (If your clients consist of other organizations, write profiles of the businesses, or of the individuals you expect to be the primary decision makers, whether they're office managers, boutique owners, or spa owners. And if you're targeting couples or families, write up each member, and identify which one is the person you need to persuade to buy from you.) Ideally you should have two or three categories; in a pinch you may want up to five, but make sure you can clearly state which one or two are the most important.

Now comes the fun part: fleshing out your profiles.

Give each one a name (first names'll do, although you get bonus points for full names) and an age. Then get to work filling in all the salient details that will turn them from two-dimensional demographics into proper characters: their hometown, occupation, housing situation, pets (if any), favorite movies/magazines/music/clothes, the stuff they carry around (in pockets, handbags, or in their car), what they read, what they do for fun, their exercise habits, and so on. You may want to supplement your personas with magazine-clipping collages, sketches, or anything else that helps you work out the fine details of your target customers. Last but not least, identify the key selling points for your product or service; why would they choose you over your competitors?

Your target market personas are your stand-ins for actual customers; down the road, when you have some real live customers, you can simply survey them to find out whether you're reaching the people you're aiming for. But in the early stages, you can keep your market personas on hand to help you review your product lines (which one will be Lisa's favorite?), your marketing materials (what will Bruce be looking for on the website?), and even your mission statement (how would Theresa react to that bit about "global reach"?).

Keep these lovelies in the same place as your mission statement—you'll want to refer to them often!

REACH, MEET GRASP

Sad though it may be, no one is universally popular. And the same is true for businesses. Although it may seem at times like there are businesses where everybody's a customer, ask yourself whether that's really true. If everyone shopped at IKEA, then there'd be no point in anyone owning antique shops or designing new furniture. Not only that, but IKEA's target market simply isn't—and can't be—"everyone." Rather, they're focused on budget-conscious shoppers who enjoy contemporary design and who are prepared to puzzle through vaguely helpful Swedish line drawings to save a bit of cash. They may have a huge market reach, but there are still plenty of holdouts who buy their furniture from artisans, second-hand shops, garage sales, and local retailers.

No matter how broad your target market is, its members share some qualities that aren't universal; your task is to identify what those qualities are. Maybe they're environmentally conscious, or perhaps they're bonded by their love of quilting. Figure out the common threads, and you have the makings of a target market profile.

❧ Navigating Change

Of course, none of this is written in stone—in fact, you may find that reevaluating becomes necessary after the first few months, or a couple of years. Your product and service offerings will probably shift over time, as will your core customer base, but that's exactly why these questions are so important; the more clearly you can answer the questions "What does your business do?" and "Who are your customers?" now, the more obvious it will be to you when those things begin to shift, and that will be a sign to you that it's time to reevaluate other things, like your prices, how you're marketing yourself, possibly even your location. And if you're anything like us, you may find that you start out believing that your target market is one thing (in our case, small nonprofits and women-run businesses) and it will turn out to expand into something quite different (perhaps encompassing large companies and the odd real estate developer). But that's all part of the adventure, isn't it?

We make a habit of evaluating these two big questions at least once a year (usually on the anniversary of our first day in business), which helps us to clarify our financial, sales, and marketing goals for the months ahead. Depending on the cycles of your business, you may want to check in on them more often.

❧ *I Love It When a Plan Comes Together*

You've just assembled the most flavorful ingredients of your business plan—your brand, niche, customer base, and mission statement. These are the core of your business, and along with the visioning work you did in Chapter 1, they'll inform every decision you make from here on in. Next, we're going to throw them on the fire and see how they hold up against reality—the financial kind.

CHAPTER 3

Financial Scenarios

Let's be honest: this is the part most of us dread. Not because we're the types who believe "math is hard" (that's the first and last time we'll be quoting Barbie, by the way), but because it simply feels a bit boring compared to all the plush-chairs-and-sugarplums visions we've been playing with up until now. However, money is the juice that will fuel many of your most exciting ventures, from paying yourself (and anyone else who may be working with you) to bringing on staff, expanding your premises, or hey, giving yourself that raise you know you deserve!

We promise to make this chapter as fun as humanly possible—but there was a time, just before we started our business, when we didn't really believe money talk could ever be fun. The root of the problem was that both of us grew up with preconceptions about money that went something like this: "Money is for greedy, rich people. *We* don't need (much) money because we're thrifty, noble, and smart. And if somebody gave us a whole bunch of money someday, I guess we could come up with some clever ways to spend it, but it's simply distasteful to spend your life in pursuit of a greasy buck."

One day a dear friend of ours pointed out that there was a whole mess of myths holding up that pile of preconceptions. One was that *there's only so much to go around.* We both happen to have grown up in families where money was on the tight side, so it's easy to see where that assumption came from. But when we were forced to really look at that belief, we realized we were unconsciously limiting ourselves to low-income, subsistence-based lives—and all due to sheer lack of imagination. We literally *couldn't imagine* making more than around $50,000 a year, because our parents had never made more than that. Besides, if we made that kind of money, where would it all go?

The answer to that question came when we met people whose personal wealth was being put to good use. And we don't mean people giving every red cent to charity, although that's a perfectly lovely thing to do. Rather, we gradually realized that making a decent living was the best way to get ourselves into a position to afford to pursue some of our personal dreams—as well as contribute to our favorite charities and good causes.

Beyond your personal solvency, of course, we also want to make sure your business has its costs covered, and then some. Although we are firm believers that money isn't the only thing that makes a business run, it's one of the main ingredients, and you won't get far if you don't have concrete goals and a good idea of how to meet them.

This chapter is about finding a way to make your dreams a reality, and while we know some of those dreams (such as escaping your oppressive boss) don't necessarily require financial backing, others (like paying rent on a charming storefront, or getting some decent health insurance) have a price tag attached. We're going to walk you through the latter, and we'll see if we can't make it relatively painless.

> *There was one other thing that motivated us to get off our butts and get passionate about our finances, and that was our indepen-dent natures. (You might guess those natures also had something to do with our wanting to be our own bosses, and you'd be right.) One day, I—this is Lauren speaking here—decided to figure out what ex-actly an RRSP (the Canadian version of a 401[k]) was, and took a book out of the library called* She Laughed All the Way to the Bank. *One idea that book puts forward is the "White Knight Syndrome," which the author believes represents many women's assumptions about money—namely, that one day we will get mar-ried and finances will become our husbands' responsibility.*
>
> *Now, although I love many, many things about that book, this particular bit really got my knickers in a twist, because that is pretty much the exact opposite of my belief about money; I'm a fiercely independent person. (I mean, for starters, I'm not exactly the type to give my boyfriend unconditional control over the TV remote, let alone hand over the checkbook.) And that was just the jump start I needed to get my financial act in gear: I realized that if I was going to hang on to my pride, I'd need to learn a few things about money, and get over a bunch of my hang-ups.*

❈ Budget-o-rama

Oh, there's just no way to make "budget" a fun word, is there? (Well, unless you're like Emira and you *looooove* a good spreadsheet.) Nevertheless, we imagine you don't have a screaming aversion to the idea of knowing how much money you're going to be earning and spending. (If you do, please consider hiring an accountant to help you with this part, or bringing aboard a business partner who enjoys num-ber crunching. This is crucial stuff.) This is the part where you figure out things like what you're going to need to charge in order to recoup your costs, pay your rent, and make a living.

Creating a budget is less daunting than you might think. It's really nothing more than a list of categories, with a dollar figure assigned to each one. You can write yours down on a napkin, if you like. We prefer spreadsheets, but we're geeks like that. (Plus we like that they do the calculations automatically—it reduces those pesky "forgot to carry the one" problems.)

If spreadsheets don't give you a case of the howling fantods, this would be a good time to fire up the computer and get ready to plug in some numbers. (If on the other hand you're more of a paper-and-pencil person, grab your notepad and—unless you're a math whiz—a calculator. One way or another, you're going to need to make some notes.) We're going to cover several basic financial planning tools for your business: your start-up budget, a budget for your ongoing costs, pricing calculations, and income projections. Did we lose you there? Don't worry, they only *sound* intimidating.

❀ Start Me Up

First things first . . . You are most likely going to have a certain number of start-up costs: one-time cash outlays to get your business going, from printing off business cards to buying a computer (or fabric, or whatever the raw materials of your products and services are). Let's get started by itemizing your start-up costs. (Ongoing costs, like rent, salaries, phone bills, and so on will all come a bit later.)

Every business is going to have a different start-up budget, but there are some broad categories that most of us have in common. To begin with, have a look through the categories below, and make a note of the items you'll need in each category. Don't worry yet about assigning specific dollar amounts to each item—you may know what some of them are now, but others will require a bit of research. For now, let's concentrate on just getting a more or less complete list of what it is you need. (You may want to mark this section up—feel free to circle or highlight the bits that apply to you, or scribble in the margins.)

So: Here are some categories to get you started. Depending on the nature of your business, you may need to spend money on the following:

RAW MATERIALS

Here you'll want to set yourself up with the minimum (or maybe a little more than what you think you'll need, just in case) materials to see yourself through your first run of work. In our case, we needed to buy one computer (we already had one), a desk, and some software. You may need a new camera and a scanner, or a barber's chair and some brushes and scissors. We're talking about the basics that will see you through a day's work, so you may want to spend just a little more for quality products with decent warranties. (If coming up with a whack of cash right at the start is too much of a challenge, see if you can buy secondhand, or lease some of these materials. Just remember, if you delay these costs by leasing, you'll need to account for the ongoing expenses in your operating budget later.)

MARKETING MATERIALS

We'll be talking about the details of marketing materials in Chapter 6, but for now, give yourself a rough budget for what you think you can afford to spend on business cards, brochures, advertising, and so on. If you're running a mail-order business, you'll want to allot some cash for your catalog, order forms, and invoices; on the other hand, if you're a one-woman consulting agency, business cards and some lunch money (for treating a few prospective clients to soup and a sandwich) may be all you need.

LEGAL STUFF

Check with your local government small business office to find out what you're legally required to do to run a licensed business. Budget for items like registering your name (and possibly trademarking it, if you're planning on being the next big record label or lipstick brand), permits, health inspections, and incorporating (which isn't for everyone, but you should look into it just in case and find out if it's a good idea—check our resource guide for more information).

RENOVATIONS

Those of you heading into retail—or any other area where your customers will be stepping off the sidewalk and into your space—will likely want to budget for personalizing your home base. If you're doing anything so extensive that a trip to the hardware store—and a favor called in to that pal who spent a summer on a construction site— won't cut it, get at least three quotes from contractors (and pad the one you pick by a good 50 percent just to be safe—renos *never* come in on time or on budget).

Got your list of start-up costs? Now it's time for some more research. You're going to need to come up with some estimated costs for all those items. You can start by doing some research online into the hard costs of some of your materials, for things like computers and furniture. Then you'll need to estimate costs for things like a security deposit, a phone, and business cards. To get those figures, either call around to leasing agents, phone companies, and printers or ask friends doing a similar level of business what they're paying. (Remember, you really only need rough figures in here, and typically we'd recommend overbudgeting a bit so you don't have any nasty surprises.)

Your start-up budget might look like this (but remember, your categories and costs are going to be unique to your business):

Raw Materials:

- Computer: $1,500
- Software: $1,000
- Printer: $350
- Phone: $150

Marketing Materials:

- Business cards: $250

Legal Stuff:

- Name registration: $50
- Business license: $100

Renovations/Office Setup:

- Furniture: $1,500
- Paint: $200
- Security deposit: $500
- Miscellaneous: $300

Now that you have a rough dollar figure for each item, add 'em all up, and you've got a pretty good idea how much cash you're going to need before you get started. If the total threatens to give you a heart attack, you may be a candidate for start-up capital. Let's talk this through a bit.

If you're finding the start-up costs a bit daunting, and there are some items you think you can live without for a little while, set a time frame for purchasing them. That way, you can get an idea of how much you'll need to earn in that span of time in order to afford the stuff you need. So if your pottery studio can only last six months at most without a bigger kiln, be sure to cost out the price of the one you want, and work that into your budget for ongoing expenses. (More on that in a couple of pages.)

❄ *Helping Hands*

First and foremost, let's remember how resourceful you are: Whether you intend on financing your start-up with credit cards, family loans, or your own savings, we're sure you can whittle the major costs into digestible chunks. If not, and after exploiting all your self-financing options, you still come up short, you may need to look into getting some financial assistance from a bank, credit union, or investor.

The number one challenge with going this route is that you will almost definitely need to write a formal business plan to qualify for a loan, which is a time-consuming and heavy-duty kind of endeavor. However, presumably if you require the kind of funding only banks can give, then we're talking about thousands of dollars, and it's well worth your putting in a few hours in front of the computer.

The great thing about writing a business plan is that by the end of it, you should have an inside-and-out, backward-and-forward understanding of your business's financial needs, which will serve you well when it comes to paying back that loan (and yes, even those "angel" investors want their money back with interest). This subject goes well beyond the scope of this book, though, so we would urge you to check out the resource guide for some tips on other sources for how to write a business plan.

Back to that fierce independence thing we brought up earlier in the chapter . . . While that's a quality that will serve you well as an entrepreneur, it can also trip you up—and when it comes to money, it definitely walks the line between help and hindrance. When you're looking at amassing your start-up capital, it's great to do it all yourself on the credit you've already got available to you, but don't be so stubborn that you let your independence literally cost you—in the form of high interest.

It may not be as instant as pulling out the charge card, but take a deep breath and go to the bank to see if you can't get a line of credit, or a cheaper cash injection. Save the credit cards, whenever possible, for purchases you know you can pay off fairly quickly. That said, we know many a gal who financed her business on credit cards in the early days—they're an especially tempting option for us women, given that we still regularly face discrimination at the bank loans desk, and that our initial financial investments tend to be lower than male entrepreneurs'—and if that is truly the only option before you, then by all means take it. But remember: You're going to pay a premium for that fast and easy money. Credit card companies' raison d'être is to keep their customers indebted, and as a result, credit card debt can be one of the toughest debts to get rid of.

As you start your business up, you'll find yourself making a lot more trips to the bank. Whether you're picking up checks or applying for a serious loan, you'll find the ATM just doesn't cut it anymore for your banking needs. Finding a business banker who will take you seriously and give you strategic advice is like finding a best friend with a backyard pool in August. While you may be tempted to stick with the bank where you had your very first savings account, take the time to shop around. Make appointments and meet with account managers until you find someone who takes you seriously.

❧ The Myth of Write-offs

Before we dive into your ongoing expenses budget, we'd like to take a small detour to discuss tax write-offs (a.k.a. tax-deductible expenses). One of the many things you'll get accustomed to as an entrepreneur is the sound of the phrase, "Oh well, you can write it off."

Nonentrepreneurs like to chant this to business owners as though it means that someone else entirely is footing the bill. As in: "Well, you can buy lunch—it's a write-off, isn't it?"

Although it's true that the government will allow you to claim some purchases against your business income (that's what your expense budget is for, after all), that doesn't mean they swoop down and pick up the check! The way it works is this: For every legitimate business expense you claim (which means you need to keep track of all the receipts), they take that amount and subtract it from the gross income your business brings in, resulting in a slightly smaller amount of income that you have to pay tax on at the end of the year.

The other thing about write-offs is that you should always check with your local small business office or your bookkeeper to see whether you can write things off at all. For instance, some people track their car and gas expenses, but if you don't need a car to do your job, you'll most likely be out of luck trying to claim those items. And although lots of self-employed people keep every last restaurant receipt they come in contact with, unless you can truthfully claim those meals as work related, they won't pass muster as "entertainment expenses."

Cinnamon Cooper had her bookkeeper write up a list of legitimate, deductible expense categories for her company, Poise bags, so that when she's considering a purchase, she can make an informed decision about whether or not it can be run through the business. Moreover, she says, "My bookkeeper's goal is, make everything fit into one of those categories, so you can deduct as much as you can." In other words, wherever possible, make sure your business expenses fall into deductible categories—and minimize the amount of cash you spend on nondeductible items.

Many uninitiated folks (or those who have questionable tax practices, who will one day be very sorry if the audit fairy comes a-knockin' on their door) treat write-offs like they are free money, and we understand that it is a pretty seductive fairytale to put your faith in, but sadly it just isn't true. So make sure you understand how you are using your write-offs so you don't end up with a big surprise at the end of the year when it's time to pay income tax—in spite of all the fabulous shoes you bought for "client meetings."

❀ *Keeping Afloat: Ongoing Expenses*

Now that you've got a handle on your start-up costs, let's talk about the recurring costs that will be the mainstays of the "expenses" column on your cash-flow sheet. As the core expenses for your company, these items will largely determine your pricing—how much you need to charge to recoup your costs (and hopefully have a bit left over for extras).

Just as we did with your start-up budget, we're going to start by creating an itemized list of categories. The dollar amounts can come later. The categories are going to vary widely depending on the kind of business you're running, but here's a rough list to get you started:

OVERHEAD

This is a term that gets bandied about a lot, but here's how we're using it: to cover the stuff that keeps a roof over your head (get it?). So: rent, phones, heating and electricity, fire and theft insurance, and so on.

PAYROLL

Figure out what you'll be paying yourself (and anyone who'll be working with you). Remember that as a business owner, it's your responsibility to pay income tax for yourself and your employees, as well as Social Security (a.k.a. FICA) tax, Medicare tax, and unemployment taxes (both federal and state). All of these taxes are based on a percentage of income, so you need to budget for your gross pay (i.e., your salary *plus* taxes—we'll cover this a little later in this chapter); this is a major perspective shift if you're used to getting your pay stubs with all the deductions neatly subtracted for you.

STAFF BENEFITS

If the "staff" equals you, and you alone, you may think you can get by without bonuses and perks—think again! If you're leaving a job that offered you health and dental benefits, look into the costs of replacing that privately, and work that into your budget. (Believe it or not, it'll be harder in the long run if you procrastinate and tell yourself you'll "work up to it.") You should also look into disability insurance (which can be pricey) and anything else you've been getting from your employer until now (from a prepaid bus pass to 401[k] matching)—or just wishing for!—and ask yourself what it will cost to provide yourself with those things in your new role.

COST OF GOODS SOLD

If you're making or selling products, you need to factor in the hard costs associated with the goods you're selling, whether it's pillow forms, fabric and thread, or the accessories you'll be selling at the front counter of your consignment store. Basically, this is the category for everything that you need to spend money on in order to be able to sell your stuff. For service-oriented businesses, this is usually less of an issue, although there still may be some cost associated with the delivery of your service, from long-distance phone bills to bike tune-ups for your fleet of couriers. For our business, website hosting, domain registration, stock photography, and fonts fall into this category. But for a retail store, it would primarily involve the cost of keeping inventory on the shelves.

CAPITAL EXPENSES

You'll have covered most of this stuff in your start-up budget, but you may want to include a line in your budget for repairing, upgrading, or replacing key equipment, since it's likely that something or other will break once a year or more. You may just want to make this a percentage of your start-up equipment costs. So if you think you'll likely need a new computer every three years, calculate one-third of the price of a new one, and add it to your annual budget; that way, by the time year three rolls around, you should have the cash set aside.

PROFESSIONAL SERVICES

If nothing else, you will likely need occasional assistance from a lawyer and/or an accountant; some businesses will require more professional help than others. If you're creating a product, you may need legal advice on a regular basis, to keep your copyright safe and possibly even to protect you from lawsuits.

TAXES

In addition to payroll taxes, you may need to pay city, state, and federal corporate taxes. This will depend on many factors, including whether or not you're incorporated, and where you do business. We recommend finding a good accountant or tax consultant to help you sort out where all your tax obligations lie—though you can also seek out information online, through www.irs.gov and via your municipal and state government websites.

MEMBERSHIPS AND SUBSCRIPTIONS

If you're in a line of work where you need to keep up-to-date on what your colleagues are up to—or even if you're just planning on doing some networking and market research—you may need to budget for membership fees in professional associations, and/or subscriptions to a few magazines or newsletters. For some of you (massage therapists, for example), professional association memberships can be critical— they're your key to being taken seriously by your clients—so make sure you're aware of the costs of keeping your membership current.

QUARTER TIME

When we're creating our annual budgets, we like to have a column for recurring monthly items, followed by four columns for quarterly totals. That's because there are some expenses in our business that come up at specific points in the year, and it's helpful to track how our expenses vary over the course of the year. For example, our financial year-end is in September, so we know that come September and October, it'll be time to pay our accountant for her work putting together the year's financial statements. It's also a helpful way to track one-time expenses like traveling to conferences, buying new equipment, or sending out Valentine's Day cards to your beloved customers.

❀ Calculating Your Salary

We've got a whole chapter devoted to this (see Chapter 10), but in brief, we want to urge you to pay yourself a decent wage. There are many reasons for this, but first and foremost, if you won't pay yourself what you're worth, who will? The first year or two may require some personal sacrifice, but it won't be long before you get tired of scraping by. Remember, your salary is now in your own hands, so this is your opportunity to pay yourself enough to live well.

Although we recognize that your salary may not seem like a high priority when you're starting out—especially when you put it alongside your other financial obligations—it's important to remember that the primary difference between your work life and your downtime is that the former should be helping you pay your bills. If it's not, then you may need to adjust your pricing so that you're able to write yourself a decent paycheck. Chiropractor Dr. Beverley Steinhoff put it this way: "Any time you take time away from your creative and family pursuits, it's business—that's how I look at it. And you have to take a real bottom line approach to that. If your business—whatever it is—can't adequately compensate you for your time, which is your most valuable resource, then you need to change your business model."

Are we sounding insistent? Well, that's because we've seen too many entrepreneurs make mistakes when it comes to their pay, and end up underpaying themselves for years (at which point, it can be hard to make the necessary changes to your business's financial structure). Watch out for these common pitfalls of the self-employed:

- *Paying yourself out of whatever's left at the end of the month:* Although there are times this is unavoidable, we decided early on to apply for an overdraft on our bank account so that we could pay ourselves a regular salary regardless of the vagaries of our cash flow. Calculate your salary based on your income and expense projections, and pay it like any other bill; otherwise you won't get an accurate picture of your business's financial health. Your business should be able to provide you with a predictable income.

- *Forgetting about your taxes:* After all your hard work, the last thing you want is to be zapped with a surprise tax bill you can't afford. No matter how paltry your pay, you'll be grateful in the long run if you set up a separate savings account (preferably one that's hard to get at, or that penalizes you for early withdrawal of funds) and funnel away a percentage of everything you earn. (In our first couple of years we ballparked our taxes by socking away 25–30 percent of our gross income, but of course the percentage will vary widely depending on your location and how much you're earning. If you're self-employed, but not incorporated, the IRS will require you to pay "estimated taxes" quarterly; don't worry, they have forms to help you estimate what you're going to owe in advance.) In the end, if you're consistent about keeping your tax money aside, you'll probably get a refund (or a less-than-you-budgeted-for tax bill) and you can treat the difference as fun money! The same goes for state and city taxes, by the way: Keep the money you collect separate from your checking account (or if that's not possible, track it carefully so you know your "real" balance). The government wants that money back.

- *Mixing up your government dues:* One of the unfortunate things about being a business owner is that you end up paying twice as much Social Security tax (because you will be paying both the employer's and the employee's portions). For nonincorporated, self-employed people, there's a comparable tax called Self-Employment Tax that applies to all your self-employment income. Consult an expert and make sure you won't get any unwelcome surprises when tax time arrives.

- *Neglecting to budget for a raise:* Try standing outside yourself and asking yourself what you'd expect to be paid for the work you intend to be doing, if you weren't the one footing the bill. Then think about what you'd expect in terms of an annual raise. If your starting salary has to be low in order for you to get the business up and running (a likely scenario), set up a five-year plan to get yourself to your target salary—and make sure you've accounted for the fact that five years from now, the cost of living will have increased.

Please, we beg you: Do your part to reduce the male-female wage gap, and budget yourself a nice, comfortable paycheck. You never know—if enough of us do it, we might just change the world a little (or a lot).

❀ *Back to Business*

Okay, you should have your budget categories itemized; now it's time to plug in your dollar figures. As with your start-up budget, this may require some research, so by all means ask around and get some ideas of what you're likely to spend in each category.

In the process of itemizing your ongoing expenses, you'll also be providing yourself with the information you need to establish your pricing structure, so we'll touch on that in this next section as well. Let's start by looking at a couple of examples to give you an idea of how your expenses will pan out. We'll look at a consulting business first, because the expense structure is simpler; next, we'll review a more complex, product-based example.

❀ *Getting Paid for Your Time*

In consultancies and other businesses where your clients pay you for your time (from graphic design to hairstyling to law), the math is fairly straightforward, because your expenses tend to be relatively simple. (Okay, hair salons need to factor in the cost of coloring products, shampoo, and so on, but for now let's focus on the time-based part of the equation.)

Let's run through a sample budget for a research consultancy; let's say it's a one-person shop.

Sample Budget: Mears and Associates (a one-person consultancy)		
Item	Cost	Annual Total (for year one)
Start-up Costs: security deposit ($500); furniture ($1,500); computer, software, printer, and phone ($3,000); paint ($200); miscellaneous ($300)	$5,500	$5,500
Overhead	$660/mo.	$7,920
Payroll (starting salary)	$45,000/yr.	$45,000
Benefits (health insurance, 401[k] "matching")	$550/mo.	$6,600
Cost of Goods Sold	n/a	$0
Capital Expenses (replacing equipment as needed)	$800/yr.	$800
Professional Services (tax preparation)	$250/yr.	$250
Sales Tax	n/a (no sales tax required on consulting services)	$0
Corporate Taxes	n/a (company is a sole proprietorship, so all income is taxed as owner's personal income)	$0
Memberships and Subscriptions	$500/yr.	$500
Total		$66,570

With $66,570 in annual expenses, what will you need to charge by the hour to meet your budget? You may be thinking, *That's easy! I just take fifty-two weeks a year, times forty hours a week . . .* PLEASE JUST STOP RIGHT THERE.

Now then: Let's talk about how much *billable* time you are going to be able to work. We're going to take a few weeks out of the year, for starters—let's say two weeks' vacation, two weeks to account for federal holidays, and another two weeks for just-in-case scenarios like sick days, emergency vet trips, and so on. So we're down to forty-six weeks in the year that you're going to work (and that's a pretty measly vacation allotment—but we're assuming you'll be making a few sacrifices in the early years).

In terms of hours per week, you may well be a solid forty-hour-a-week worker, but there's no way you'll be billing every minute of your time. For starters, you'll be checking email, answering the phone, and traveling to meetings. Then there's the administrivia of running your business: Between marketing, doing sales work, invoicing, and ordering stamps, your number of available hours dwindles rapidly. One pretty solid standard to use for most consultancy-type businesses is to aim for 60–65 percent of your time to be billable. (If you can boost that number, that's fabulous—but we've never met an entrepreneur who could manage over 75 percent of working time as billable without making serious sacrifices on the actual making-sure-the-business-is-healthy side.)

In your first year of business, you're likely to end up on the lower end of the billable-time spectrum, because you'll be working hard to drum up business (and probably won't be booked solid). Let's say you're billing 50 percent of your time in year one—that's 20 hours a week, 46 weeks a year . . . 920 hours. Going back to your $66,570 figure, we divide it by 920, and we get $72.36—that's the hourly rate you'll need to charge in order to break even. Let's bump that up to $75 an hour (a nice, round number) to give you a little extra cushion.

Does that sound like a lot? Well, ask around and find out what other people in your field are charging. Chances are, if they're self-employed, it will be something in that neighborhood—if they're charging less, they may be undercharging, or they may simply have lower costs than you're budgeting for. But don't get too hung up on what other people are charging; after all, the real test is whether or not your clients are willing to pay what you're asking. And chances are, if you're good at what you do, and charging a fair price, they won't bat an eyelash.

Remember, just because you were *earning* $20 an hour at your old job doesn't mean that's what your employer was *charging* for your time; after all, your salary was only one of the many expenses we outlined above. We've found this is one of the biggest leaps new entrepreneurs need to make: getting comfortable with just how much you're worth. (Hint: quite a lot, actually.)

> On top of the bare-bones budget you've put together, you may want to compile a wish list of things you'd like to buy when you've had some success. Write down the things you imagine as part of your fantasy "successful entrepreneur" life . . . a bright, sunny office; beautiful stationery; fancy computers; a company car; annual staff retreats on the Oregon coast; and so on. Then jot down a rough cost estimate next to each one—so you know how much you'll need to earn to realize those dreams. Not only are you more likely to achieve goals you've taken the time to articulate and write down, but you'll also have something to fall back on when you exceed your revenue targets.

One final note before we move on to our next example: The nice thing about our $75-an-hour rate is that in year two, you stand to make a higher salary without needing to increase your hourly rate—just by increasing your number of billable hours (which should happen naturally, as word spreads about your fabulous service). If you can get up to 60 percent billable time in your second year, you'll have an additional $16,000+ in gross income, which you can use to give yourself a raise, buy yourself a few "wish list" items, or just sock away for a rainy day.

> *There are a whole lot of people out there who seem to think it's not only interesting but unavoidable to work more than forty hours a week. Aside from that being a radically unhealthy approach, it's also totally unsustainable from a business point of view. If you find that you're unable to make ends meet without regularly working twelve-hour days, six or seven days a week, ask yourself if your business can actually sustain itself in the long run. After all, if your business depends on you being overworked, can you really afford to keep it going?*

❈ The Means of Production

If your business falls into the retail or product-oriented category (i.e., the stuff you are selling involves hard costs), you have a more complex budget situation, because you need to account for cost of goods sold, inventory management, and profit margins. You're also going to be assessing your income based on gross and net sales, rather than on billable hours. Given the amount of jargon in this paragraph, we're going to detour into a few definitions before we jump into the number crunching.

- *Cost of goods sold (COGS):* In short, the price you're paying for the stuff you want to sell, whether it's raw materials (e.g., wood, nails, and hinges) or products for resale (like the drums and guitars you'll be stocking in your music shop). Don't forget to include the price of packaging! We'll talk more about COGS in just a sec.

- *Inventory:* The cost of having stuff sitting around for the length of time it takes to sell it. Great big CD stores have much higher inventory costs because they need to keep many copies of the high-selling discs on hand, as well as stocking less-popular albums for one-stop shoppers. One of the main reasons stores have seasonal sales is to clear out old inventory (thus recouping the cost of purchasing them in the first place) and make room for the new.

- *Profit margin:* The difference between your sale price and your COGS. If you paid $6 for a pair of barrettes and sold them for $10, your profit margin is $4—easy peasy.

- *Gross sales:* The total dollar figure of sales you make in a given time period—say, a month. If you sold a hundred pairs of barrettes at $10 a pair, your gross sales would be $1,000.

- *Gross profit on sales:* Basically this is your profit margin multiplied by the number of products sold. Using the hundred pairs of barrettes example, your gross profit on sales would be $4 times 100 pairs, or $400. (However, you're likely to sell other stuff besides barrettes, so your calculations will probably be a bit more complex.)

The biggest difference between product-oriented and service-based businesses is that rather than basing your budget on billable hours, you'll be using your gross profit on sales projections. You are also more likely to have higher overhead, start-up, and ongoing costs, because you need to make sure you've got enough inventory on hand to keep your customers coming back.

❈ *Figuring Out COGS and Pricing*

This is a pretty complex topic, so although we're going to give you some basic tips here, please be aware that there are lots of resources around to help you figure out the right price for your product. However, we'd be remiss if we didn't say a thing or two about how to get from your cost of goods sold (COGS) to the price your customer (whether wholesale or retail) ends up paying.

First off, even if you are setting up a retail shop (online or offline) to sell your wares, remember that down the road you may end up with opportunities to wholesale your product. Wholesale customers will expect to pay about half of retail price, and they'll also expect that price to be negotiable based on quantities. (If they're placing a large order, they'll want a deeper discount.) When that day comes, if you haven't factored in a wholesale pricing structure, you may find yourself selling a whole bunch of product at little to no profit to you. So lesson number one is to set your wholesale price first, *then* your retail price.

To determine your COGS, itemize all the direct costs involved in creating your product. This should include both materials and labor—but only the labor involved in the manufacture of the goods. Marketing, sales, and so on should be covered by your profit margin. (We'll talk about that shortly.)

Say your company makes vinyl bags. Your COGS should include all your materials (vinyl, thread, clips, straps, zippers, Velcro, labels, lining fabric, hang tags, and everything else you need to make a bag), as well as labor costs for the time it takes to sew a bag. Let's say your materials cost you $12 a bag. (Don't skimp on this—in fact, it's always good to pad this figure a little to account for unforeseen costs. If your cheap zipper hookup skips town, you don't want to have to absorb the increased cost of picking up some emergency zippers at the local sewing-supply store.) Now we need to add on labor costs. That means we need to translate your annual salary to an hourly wage.

First, let's figure out how many hours you'll work in a year. We'll assume you'll work 46 weeks (if you skipped the last section, flip back a few pages to see how we came up with that figure), 40 hours a week. And 46 weeks ✗ 40 hours/week = 1,840 hours. Now, take your annual salary—let's say it's $40,000 a year—and divide it by 1,840 to get your hourly wage: $40,000 ÷ 1,840 = $21.74/hour.

(See why a spreadsheet makes this easier?)

Let's say it takes you thirty minutes to stitch up a bag. (Remember not to underestimate your time—even the time it took to replace that broken sewing machine needle counts. Give yourself a margin of error so that your COGS is a reflection of real life.) Your labor costs per bag would be half of $21.74, or $10.87. Add that to your $12 in materials, and your COGS comes to $22.87.

There are as many different approaches to setting your wholesale and retail prices as there are self-proclaimed business experts, but here's a simple one that works pretty darned well:

★ To determine your wholesale price, take your COGS and double it. (Using our example, that would be $22.87 ✗ 2 = $45.74.)

★ Your retail price should be double your wholesale price ($45.74 ✗ 2 = $91.48).

That's right: **Your retail price must be four times your cost of goods.** We can't emphasize this enough. We've seen too many small business owners shoot themselves in the foot by underpricing their products.

There's a little leeway there, obviously. You may want to round your figures up or down a little, so you might set your bag's retail price at $89.99 or $95. Just don't go reducing your prices (especially your wholesale prices) by more than 1 or 2 percent without thinking long and hard about it, because that 1 percent can make a big, big difference when you're selling hundreds of items. In fact, you may want to err on the high side when setting your wholesale price, because it will give you some room to move when big wholesalers ask for special consideration.

In the end, though, you should end up with a wholesale price that gives you enough gross profit that you can cover your non-COGS costs—overhead, marketing, and all that other good stuff we've been discussing (like your salary, for instance, since only a portion of your time is going to go into manufacturing).

❀ *Whoa, Nelly!*

If your retail price seems high, you have a couple of options. One is to make sure everyone knows just how special your product is, and convince them to pay a little more for the privilege of owning a Miss Thang original. (We'll talk about this a little more toward the end of this chapter.) Another option is to revisit your COGS and see if you can reduce your up-front costs. (If your retail price is simply too high to be reasonable—i.e., if you're sure no one will pay that much—you will most certainly need to bring down your COGS.)

So how do you reduce your COGS? Well, that's going to depend a lot on your business. Hannah Howard of Lizzie Sweet prefers to use essential oils whenever possible to scent her luscious bath and body products, but since fragrance oils are less expensive, she's chosen to use those instead for certain products, to keep her line of products affordable to the average consumer. She's still very quality-conscious, but since it's just as important to her to keep her prices within reach of everyday working women, she makes an effort to source materials that help keep her COGS down while still respecting the environment and her customers' health.

Another way to cut down on COGS is to negotiate better wholesale prices with *your* suppliers. If you're buying a ton of vinyl every year, you should be eligible for a better price than your local fabric store can offer. A few well-placed phone calls can make a world of difference to your expenses.

❀ *Add It Up*

All right: Now that you know how to calculate your COGS, your wholesale price, and your retail price, let's review a sample budget for a two-person company making vinyl bags and selling them in a small storefront. We're going to start with a budget that doesn't include COGS. You'll see why in a few moments.

You may be wondering why, after all this time we've spent talking about COGS, we've gone and left it out of the budget. Seems like an important budget item, right? Well, absolutely. The trouble is, we can't calculate the total COGS until we know how many bags our friends need to sell in a year in order to pay for the above-listed expenses.

Take the total expenses on page 69—that's $136,750. That's their total expenses for the year (excluding COGS, of course), so at a minimum, they'll need to bring in that much revenue to cover costs.

Now, since our gals are going to be selling these bags at retail prices, we'll calculate our profit margin per bag using the retail price, which they've rounded up to $95.00. The profit margin is calculated by subtracting the COGS from the retail price: $95 − $22.87 = $72.13. (Wondering where these numbers came from? Take a wander back to the previous section.)

You might think that we simply need to divide $136,750 by $72.13 to get the number of bags they need to sell (1,896 over the course of the year, or about 36 a week)—and you'd be right. Except that we also need to factor in the cost of unsold (and unsellable—after all, there will be a few sewing machine errors here and there) inventory. That number will vary widely from one business to another, but for our purposes we'll assume that about 20 percent of inventory will go unsold. That means that for every four bags they make and sell, they'll make one more that doesn't sell. And the cost of that fifth bag (another $22.87) will be added to their business expenses for the year.

Sample Budget: Carried Away, Inc.
(a two-person bag manufacturing company and retailer)

Item	Cost	Annual Cost
Start-up Costs: (secondhand sewing machine, minor renos for store, raw materials, incorporation)	$16,200	$16,200
Overhead	$1,800/mo.	$21,600
Payroll (starting salary x 2)	$80,000/yr.	$80,000
Benefits (health insurance, 401[k] "matching")	$1,000/mo.	$12,000
Capital Expenses	$3,000/yr.	$3,000
Professional Services (incorporation, tax preparation, trademarking)	$3,250/yr.	$3,250
Sales Taxes	n/a (taxes will be added to all prices and kept aside)	$0
Corporate Taxes	n/a (company is a limited partnership, so all income is taxed as owners' personal income)	$0
Memberships and Subscriptions	$700/yr.	$700
Total		$136,750

We can do a quick calculation by adding another 25 percent (that's the ratio of 20 percent unsold to 80 percent sold) on top of our COGS, bringing the COGS to $28.59 per bag, and the profit margin to $66.41.

Dividing $66.41 into $136,750 gives us 2,059—which is the number of bags these lovelies will have to sell in order to meet their budget. With the extra 412 unsold bags, that brings their production run for the year to 2,471, or about 206 bags a month. (Let's hope they have nimble fingers!)

❧ *Plan B*

You may be feeling like both the above examples were far too optimistic; if so, Little Miss Cautious, you're our kind of businessperson! We're compulsively pessimistic about our financial projections—firm believers that the cynic is never disappointed. Here's a special section just for you.

Once you've got a handle on what kind of income you'll need to meet your expenses, go through your budget and highlight any line items that you feel are negotiable. That might include anything from rent (if you think you can operate out of your living room for the first year), to your salary (figure out what you can live on, and label that "nonnegotiable"; the remainder can be "negotiable"), to anything you've put in place that might be optimistic (such as traveling to conferences or trade shows). Using this method, you'll be better able to navigate financial setbacks, because you'll be able to identify the places where you can cut back if absolutely necessary. We don't advocate using this as your primary plan of attack—because there's only so long you can go without those things—but it's always good to have a backup scenario in case you fall behind for a month or two.

WHEN PLAN B BECOMES PLAN A

Although we like a bargain as much as the next person, we have to admit that the cost savings you gain with a tight budget doesn't make up for the stresses of worrying about your bank balance month after month. If you've been using the Plan B approach for too long, it's time to take a look at what's not working—because after the first couple of years, you should be meeting your revenue goals and able to manage a few more expenses.

Your finances will likely be unpredictable in the early years, but make sure you're keeping on top of them, and revising your budgets regularly to reflect reality. And if your salary has been stuck for months at a level where you're selling off your prize comic book collection to make rent, it's time to look carefully at your projections and make sure they're still realistic.

Every business is different, so there aren't any hard and fast rules on this—some will require some belt tightening for the first year and then smooth out, where others will take longer to deliver rewards. But it's always worth checking in with yourself (and your business partner, if you have one) to make sure you're where you expected to be, so you don't wake up years down the road, still sacrificing all those "negotiables" that don't feel quite so negotiable anymore.

❋ *I Wanna Take You Higher*

The price you set for your products/services can often be part of your image as well, and will affect how people see you. It's worth doing a bit of research to find out what your competitors are charging so that you can decide how you want your prices to compare. (This relates to the specialization stuff we talked about in Chapter 1.) If you're going to be cheaper than the competition, then you're likely going for sales volume, or trying to reach a niche you don't think has yet been accessed (such as a lower-income demographic). If you want to set your price at a comparable level, then you need to make sure what you're selling is distinct enough in other ways so that people will choose it over other options. Or you may want to be more expensive because your brand is about developing a superior product aimed at a more exclusive audience.

Setting your price higher than others'—and delivering a superior product—will in fact cause many people to value you more. It is probably not the strategy you want to take if high volume is your goal, but it can be a very valuable approach. Just make sure your end product warrants the increased price, and that you reflect that quality in all your marketing materials. And remember: If your goods are handmade—assuming they're made well—your customers will likely perceive them as superior to (or at least more special than) machine-made goods. (The same goes for products made in small batches.)

If you have a strong portfolio of work, know that you offer better products or services than your competitors, and want to be perceived as a leader in your field, you may want to consider costing yourself above your competitors.

> ▶ When you buy a pattern from Betsy Ross, you're buying something that's a far cry from your average sewing pattern. Betsy Ross owner Aimee Dolby explains the difference: "I always include a thank-you note, and I always wrap it in gift paper. So it's like getting a present in the mail. . . . I figure for all the work that I'm putting into it—and I hand-illustrate the booklet—I can price above those other patterns. And you can also reuse mine. So I priced it at the top of the market."

TOO CHEAP TO BE TRUE?

In the consulting world, when you're submitting proposals and bidding on work, it can be very tempting to want your estimate to come in lower than the competition's, every time. And while there are certainly some clients who will always choose the cheapest provider, those may not always be the clients you want. (In fact, many clients automatically dismiss the lowest and the highest estimates, and focus on the ones in the middle.) And sometimes, being the cheapest can cast suspicion on your ability to deliver. We all get skeptical when we see those super-cheap designer shoes for sale online, and wonder if they're really as good as what's advertised. The same can go for your quote. In some cases, when it gets evaluated against others who are proven in the industry, people will suspect that you are either going to deliver substandard results or that you don't really understand the scope of the project. They can lose confidence in you and actually decide against hiring you because you didn't ask for enough money.

❀ *Timing Is Everything*

How do you decide when you can afford to spend all that money starting to build up in your bank account? The first step is to make some income projections.

Much like budgets, income projections are all about educated guesswork—they're an estimate of when your money is going to come in. For some businesses, there's no lag time between delivering your product and getting paid (hands-on service work such as massage therapy, for example). For most of us, though, there's a certain amount of waiting around for checks, either from projects or from retailers who order your goods. Here's how we do our income projections—yours will vary depending on the nature of your business, but the principles still apply.

Looking at a three-month span, we'll go through our list of projects and determine how long we expect each to take, and then plug the resulting payment schedule into our spreadsheet. For example, if a project is likely to take three months to complete, and it's billed in three installments, we'll estimate when we're likely to issue each invoice, and then add the time lapse—usually about a month—between sending out an invoice and receiving a check. (Those of you selling products wholesale will want to employ a similar method to account for your wholesale clients' payment schedules. As a rule, we've found that the bigger the client, the longer they take to issue a check. Maybe it's bureaucracy, or maybe—as some small wholesalers have complained to us—it's an abuse of their huge buying power. Either way, avoid shooting yourself in the foot by factoring in a generous lag time for big clients.)

Using the aforementioned example, we might end up with $3,500 in September, $1,500 in October, and a final payment of $3,500 in November. Doing the same for each project, we'll end up with monthly totals we can use to roughly estimate our monthly revenues.

We review our income projections every week or two so that we can adjust them as necessary. It's very much a fluid document, because project schedules are always changing. (You may also need to adjust for unforeseen circumstances like lost invoices.)

We also keep a separate column—let's call it the "once in a blue moon" column—in the spreadsheet for clients who are dragging their feet, or unlikely ever to complete their projects, so that we aren't counting on that money arriving any time soon. That way we aren't dismissing the possibility that those slower-moving projects will get us paid eventually, but we also don't have to revise our projections constantly, due to predictable project delays.

❀ *Did You Make It This Far?*

If you're still hanging in there, we salute you—you must truly have the stomach for self-employment! There's no doubt that budgeting is up there on the list of Most Headache-Inducing Activities, but in the end we're always glad to have sorted out the nuts and bolts of financial reality (even if, in the end, a budget is merely a "what-if" version of reality).

Better yet, with the money stuff out of the way, you're ready to actually set up shop. Can you stand it? Take a deep breath . . . we're about to take the big plunge.

Chapter 4

Setting Up Shop

Wʜᴇɴ ʏᴏᴜ'ʀᴇ ɪɴ ᴛʜᴇ early stages of setting up a new business, the line between planning and implementing is pretty blurry—maybe you've been printing T-shirts on the side for a year or so before you decide to make it your full-time occupation. But since we're the ones writing the book here, we're going to take the liberty of compartmentalizing. So although you may already have a few pieces of the puzzle in place, we're going to focus on the transition from dreaming up your entrepreneurial vision to making it a reality.

This "make it real" stage has three steps: First, decide on a name for your company; next, choose a location from which you'll operate; and finally, get your legal papers in order.

Once you've got those bits covered, you'll be well into reality-land and ready to open your doors to your first customer. But first things first: Let's get your shiny new shingle ready to hang.

❋ Say My Name

If you've ever been responsible for naming a pet, or a baby (or maybe an asteroid?), you know what a mixed burden and pleasure the naming process can be. There's a special delight that accompanies the knowledge that you came up with the moniker by which darling Brooklyn the wonder dog is known. When it comes to naming your business, the process is complicated a little by bureaucratic considerations, but there's still a thrilling sense of possibility that pervades the moment when you sit down to consider how you want your venture to be known to the world.

Everyone has their own way of getting creative—from group brainstorming to solitary forest walks—and that will be the heart of the naming process. We can't give you connect-the-dots instructions on how to find inspiration, but we can give you a few tips from those who've done it before, along with some principles to bear in mind as you're evaluating the candidates.

To prepare for your naming session, pull out the work you did in Chapter 2: your mission statement, target audience profiles, and notes on the personality of your business (including anything you wrote down about distinguishing yourself from the competition). All of these bits and pieces will help keep you focused as you dream up names.

Your **mission statement** will give you some useful vocabulary around your business's values, as well as some of the more concrete aspects of your products and services.

The **personality notes** lay down the parameters for the *style* of name you choose. If you want your business to be thought of as "edgy, DIY, and antiestablishment," you should probably avoid names that smack of multinational corporations or high-end law firms.

Your **target audience profiles** have the final say. When you've narrowed it down to a handful of contenders, try running them past your fictional review panel and they'll tell you which one is the frontrunner.

Your business may have simple naming needs; perhaps you're a one-person consultancy who occasionally brings in freelancers, and "Mears and Associates" will do quite nicely. (If that's the case, you may want to skim over the next couple of pages—there's no need for you to belabor the naming process.) On the other hand, if you're going into a more public line of work, such as a retail store or a restaurant, your name may pass the lips of hundreds of people a day—in which case, you'll want to take your time and consider your options carefully.

Once you've reviewed your notes, it's time to get creative. If you work better in groups, ask a couple of friends to give you a hand—otherwise, set the stage for a solo daydreaming session. Perhaps you get your best ideas in the bath; in that case, draw yourself a nice hot one and keep a notepad next to you (along with a towel to dry your hands on). Or maybe your happy place involves a bit more physical activity—a brisk jog or some gardening. Whatever you designate as your ideal setting, make it happen, and be sure to bring along your notes so you can refer back to them as you go.

The cardinal rule of brainstorming is simply this: no censoring allowed. Do your best not to pre-edit your list of ideas; simply jot down everything that comes into your mind and leave the weeding for later. Often one idea will lead to another, and the more potential names you can come up with, the clearer your direction will become.

Give yourself plenty of time with this stage, but once the well runs dry, don't be afraid to say, "That's enough." You may well have nailed down the perfect name already—so don't force yourself to list hundreds of possibilities if your gut tells you you're on track.

Now on to the culling stage: Run through your list and circle the ones that communicate your message most strongly. Tweak them, if necessary, until you've narrowed your list down to a few candidates.

If you've been going it alone so far, you may want to pause here until you can assemble a focus group to help you review the short list. This is another of those times when your friends can pitch in and make a world of difference. Getting a second opinion is key here, because after all, this will be a major facet of your public profile.

STUCK? HERE ARE A FEW QUESTIONS TO HELP YOU GET THE NAME IDEAS FLOWING:

Review your personality notes and your target market profiles. What images do you associate with them?

What names did you choose for your target audience members? (Maybe you can even name your business after one of your personas . . .)

What makes you different from the competition?

What businesses have names you love? Can you identify a pattern you might follow? (Maybe you're drawn to wordplay, or to companies with the owners' names in them.)

Other fun naming ideas we've run across:

Montreal-based eco-friendly jewelry and accessory line Rose Flash—so named after the founder's summer camp nickname.

Giddy Giddy, a California company that makes felt hair clips for young girls, was inspired by the Japanese-Hawaiian term "giri giri," which refers to a cowlick, or the little swirl in the back of a baby's hair. Owner Teri Dimalanta always loved the word, and because of the flipped "r," it sounded a little like "giddy giddy" in English.

The founders of Bring Your Own Bag, purveyors of reusable cloth tote bags, put their message right into their name. Beyond creating beautiful bags, they hope to reduce plastic bag consumption, so when it came to naming the company, they went with the direct approach.

So once you've got your pals around the table, start by giving them a few tips on the audience you're hoping to reach, and the services and products you plan to offer. (By the way, if you think you might eventually expand those products and services, you'll want to make sure your name doesn't tag you as a one-trick pony.) Then run through the finalists and open the floor to comments.

Chances are pretty high that your friends won't be unanimous on this, and that's perfectly fine—after all, you're the boss and you get final say. The point of the exercise is simply to help you talk through the pros and cons of each name with a group of folks who are a wee bit less invested in the business than you are; you need to get the perspective of a person who's hearing about you for the first time. (And if one friend hates everyone else's favorite, don't lose any sleep—you can't please everybody, and it's ultimately your call.)

Don't despair if your volunteers send you back to the drawing board; so long as they've given you some concrete input on what's working and what's not, you should have enough material to go back to the brainstorming and take another run at it. The end result will be stronger for having been carefully chosen.

When your humble authors tackled the naming process, we started by focusing on the things that distinguished us from our competitors—and the most obvious and basic of those, given our high-tech environment, was our gender. We also intended to market ourselves to other women-owned businesses, so we decided we wanted a name that evoked femininity, but subtly (because we didn't want to be typecast as girlish or high femme—after all, we knew we'd also be working with businesses and nonprofits with diverse employees and audiences).

We wanted to marry creative imagery with a descriptive phrase, so that anyone coming across our name would understand both what we do, and get a sense of how we do it. We free-associated words and phrases with a feminine (but not too feminine) flavor, until we arrived at the image of a raised eyebrow—that *trademark of 1940s film noir "dames." The arched brow communicated intelligence, humor, and a no-nonsense attitude, along with fabulous style: all the things we wanted our clients to see in us. All that remained was to tack on a descriptive "web studio"—we considered everything from "website developers" to "Internet" to "design," but arrived at "web studio" as being both specific and approachable—and our name was decided. (It also helped that a quick online search revealed that www.raisedeyebrow.com was available for purchase—a must in our line of work.)*

❊ The Perfect Spot

When you're starting out, and dreaming of the grand successes that await you, there is a temptation to go all out and spend money you don't have on "investment pieces" such as beautiful business cards and top-of-the-line equipment, and tell yourself they'll pay for themselves as long as you meet your (ambitious, of course) sales goals. These expenses seem necessary because they make you feel legitimate—like a "real" businessperson.

Please allow us to assure you that other businesspeople will consider you especially shrewd if you wait till you can afford such luxuries before spending your cash on them. (You'll also probably meet the odd blowhard who tells you that this or that expense is a must; we hope you'll spare no time dismissing any such opinion. After all, you're the only one who's thought through exactly where your spending priorities should lie.)

This lesson also applies to selecting your location. Although you may see yourself in a beautiful loft-conversion studio or a high-traffic storefront, you may be doing yourself a huge favor by starting out small. After all, rent is going to be one of your major ongoing expenses, and if you can save a few shekels by phasing in your dream location, those savings will pass directly on to you (and you can then apply the extra cash to, say, your *other* rent).

▶ One of our favorite Victoria, B.C., businesses, Smoking Lily, set up shop in a teeny-tiny store measuring four feet by eleven feet—so small that much of the merchandise had to be set out on the sidewalk out front, and only one or two customers could fit inside at a time. The minuscule boutique was the perfect showcase for Smoking Lily's carefully handcrafted, silk-screened apparel and accessories—and it also made for plenty of press coverage, since the store was the smallest one in the city. It became a destination not only for fashion lovers, but also for curious tourists and wanderers who couldn't help but poke their noses into the charming hole-in-the-wall. Years later, they added a slightly larger Vancouver location, but their personality still shines through to customers who adore the craft and sense of discovery they get from the unique and small-run pieces.

This is a great time to get creative about what you need, space-wise. Do you need room to upholster furniture? If so, you'll likely need to get your hands on some specialized equipment and a site that can contain it. But perhaps you can forego a sizable showroom for the time being, and make use of an upstairs window and a charming staircase. Obviously, everyone's needs will be different—a restaurant's location can be a make-or-break proposition, so if that's your gig, you may not want to skimp on rent—but we've seen so many creative solutions to the location question we can't resist passing them on.

If you're a consultant, you can probably make do for at least a year or two (if not more) by operating out of your home, and meeting clients in their offices (or at a nearby café); we've found that our meetings are more productive in the client's space, as it gives us a better sense of who they are and what they do (and ensures that people have fewer excuses to miss meetings). We worked for the first couple of years out of a corner of Lauren's bedroom, and our foray into "official" office space was a shared office with a print designer (prompted by the realization that our travel time to and from meetings would be cut significantly if we were within walking distance of a good chunk of our client list).

Shared space can be a great setup for many other businesses, especially those with specialized equipment. If you don't need 24/7 access to your machinery, a shared studio might be just the thing for you— ask around and see if you can find someone willing to share the cost of the equipment in exchange for limiting their use to part-time. Given all the other things you'll be managing, from finances to marketing, half-time production may be all you have time for—to begin with, anyway. We know clothing designers, woodworkers, potters, and jewelry designers who started out with this type of setup, and moved on to their own production facilities once they were confident their cash flow could support them.

If you're a product designer looking for affordable studio space, consider nontraditional venues. Hannah Howard of Lizzie Sweet rents space in a church—not exactly what she set out looking for, but it's all hers and the price is right.

Retailers may wonder how you can stray from the "location, location, location" dictum, and you're right: Foot traffic is hugely important, so you may need to splurge on a hefty lease to find just the right spot. But you can also look at emerging neighborhoods—areas where the rents haven't quite caught up to the trendier districts. Maybe you've noticed a lot of people moving into a hood that doesn't have a good video store yet, or a couple of cool galleries setting up shop a few blocks from where the prime real estate ends and the bargains begin.

The other major way to save money on retail leases is to cut back on your square footage. Another clever thing about Smoking Lily's teensy store in Victoria is the high ceilings, which allow them to hang their clothes from the walls in two tiers, one above the other.

(Yes, the clothes are out of the reach of all but WNBA players, but they simply lift down the hangers with a pole hook when a customer wants a closer look.) Perhaps your space can adopt a similarly efficient floor plan.

Those of you on the manufacturing side of things may find that when you're in production, you need double or triple your usual space just to store and organize your products. If your space can't accommodate the sheer volume of stuff, consider renting a storage locker as a short-term solution—it can act as your "warehouse" and save you paying for a bigger space before you can really afford it.

Whatever you determine to be the ideal locale for your grand opening, remember to keep an eye on the future; if you think you may be moving up to your dream space in a year or two, don't sign a long lease. (On the other hand, if you find a screaming deal on a place you love, you may want to lock in for the long haul in exchange for a better deal on the rent—just make sure you know what the penalties are for breaking your lease if you need to.)

❀ *Ye Olde Internette Shoppe*

Lest you think that we've left out "virtual" storefronts, we've saved a special section just to talk about online sales. Whether you're planning on augmenting your "brick-and-mortar" sales with online retailing, or you're going entirely dot-com, there are a few issues specific to Internet sales that you should consider before you get started.

Many of our clients who have ventured into e-commerce started out selling their merchandise wholesale, and were tempted online by the higher (than wholesale) profit margin and lower (than retail) overhead, available via direct Internet sales. It's true you can make more per item online, but make sure you've accounted for the cost of setting up your web store, as well as the additional costs associated with online merchant accounts (which allow you to accept credit cards) and the time you'll spend on packaging and shipping products all over the world. We've seen many companies overwhelmed by the amount of time and money shipping takes up when they make the switch to selling through their websites; if you aren't prepared, you may really start to hate going to the post office.

The same applies to those of you who are already doing offline retail, although if you're buying products wholesale from suppliers and reselling them, your profit margin will be a little smaller than if you were manufacturing the products yourself.

Ultimately the thing to bear in mind is that your online store will have expenses much like an offline one would: Instead of rent, you have hosting fees; in lieu of a cash register, you'll be paying a payment processor; and your website developer's pay will replace the cost of hiring sales staff. It may turn out that you'll make more money by selling online, but be careful not to buy into the e-commerce hype—doing it well isn't as cheap as some people might lead you to believe. See the resource guide for some places to get started, if e-commerce is in the cards for you.

❃ *Legal Necessities*

There are some bits of paperwork you can't do without—and unfortunately we can't list every one of them here. That's because every state and district has its own rules about the registration and licensing of businesses, so you're better off contacting your local authorities to find out what you need to do in order to be officially recognized.

Your legal to-do list may include these items:

Business License(s): It's off to City Hall for this one—usually you pay an annual license fee to operate a business, and if you're opening more than one location, you'll need a license for each one. While you're at it, check to make sure that your location of choice is zoned for the type of business you want to operate. (This is especially important for those starting out at home.) N.B. Depending on the nature of your business, you may also need a state or federal license—your local government office should be able to tell you if that's the case.

Sales Tax License: If you'll be charging sales tax (i.e., if you're operating a retail shop, or selling products directly to customers), you will need a sales tax license or permit (sometimes known as a seller's permit or a certificate of resale). Contact your state government office for details on how to obtain the proper paperwork. Note that wholesalers also need seller's permits (sometimes referred to as reseller's permits).

Partnership Agreement: If you're going into business with a partner (or multiple partners), this is a must. Don't believe us? Read the story on page 22 for a reminder of how skipping an agreement can jeopardize a good friendship.

Incorporation: This isn't for everyone, but it's well worth a visit to a lawyer to find out if the legal protection it offers is worthwhile for your business. (A good lawyer won't be afraid to turn down business if it's a waste of your time.)

Federal Tax ID: If your business is incorporated, or a partnership, and/or has employees, you will need a Federal Tax ID number (a.k.a. Employer ID number, or EIN), which you can get through the IRS.

Trademarking: As with many legal transactions, trademarking is often one of those things that don't seem necessary until it's too late. We know a number of business owners who decided to forego obtaining a trademark when they started out—frequently because there seemed like far more urgent things to spend their precious cash on during the start-up phase—but who got an unpleasant shock down the road when they discovered another business using their name (or their designs). Take it from those who've been there: It's far less expensive to trademark yourself early on than it is to undertake a legal battle later. So if your name is a crucial part of your identity—or if you're selling designs or other items that can be trademarked—consider making the investment to protect yourself. To learn more about trademarks in the United States, visit the United States Patent and Trademark Office website at www.uspto.gov—you can even file your trademarks online. For Canadians, a web search for "trademarks Canada" should bring up the website for the Canadian Intellectual Property Office, which will guide you through the bureaucratic funhouse of registering your trademark(s).

Legal Musts for Retailers: If you're running a store—either online or "brick-and-mortar"—ask your lawyer for help drafting a policy for returns and refunds. If lawyer's fees are completely beyond your budget, ask around and see if you can pick up tips from other stores. Just bear in mind that unless you have a lawyer review it, it may not hold water, and an especially horrible customer could potentially make your life pretty miserable if your policy's not legally sound. In legalese, one little word can make a whole world of difference, and trust us, you want that difference to be in *your* favor. (And hey, online retailers? Same goes for your privacy policy, which is a must if you're selling on the web.)

In short, get everything in writing. This is the point at which the formerly imaginary becomes tangible, and you're going to want everything documented for future reference. If you're a particularly pessimistic (or forgetful) type, you may want to make extra copies and file them in a safe-deposit box—or with your lawyer.

Every minute you spend on this bureaucratic stuff now will save you hours and days of headaches down the road, not to mention sleepless nights. And there's also something fun about having the government officially recognize what until now has been living inside your head (although sadly we haven't yet discovered a way to make a business license look attractive).

FINDING A LAWYER

Sure, there are some sharks out there in the legal world, but when you've got a fight on your hands, having a shark by your side can come in real handy. Trust your gut, and ask lots of questions. Here are a few tips to keep in mind when looking for a lawyer:

As with everything, word of mouth is your friend here. Ask around for referrals.

Don't be afraid to test their knowledge of your particular sub-ject area. Lawyers have specialties, so it's worth shopping around to find one that's a fit for your business. For example, when we first met our lawyer, who bills himself as an Internet law specialist, we asked a lot of questions about copyrighting online designs and soft-ware code. Although you may not be a legal expert, you may find you know enough to spot the poseurs by keeping the conversation in familiar territory.

Ask about their billing practices. They should be willing to clearly communicate their hourly fees, and how much specific ser-vices will cost, ahead of time. You should never get a bill that's a surprise.

If your work involves intellectual copyright at all (e.g., you're an artist, designer, writer, or other creative professional), you may find yourself needing a lawyer who is not only an expert on trademarks and copyright, but also willing to litigate if necessary. Not all firms are litigating firms, so you'll want to make sure you find one that is, so that your lawyer's cease-and-desist letters have some teeth.

SERVICE SWAPPING

Those of you in the DIY, crafting, or product spheres are probably very familiar with the concept of doing work in trade—a dress in exchange for a pair of earrings or two, or a coffee table in exchange for some plumbing work. The same model can function for any professional relationship, as long as both parties feel their work is being appropriately valued. So if cash is tight, see if you can track down a lawyer or an accountant who's willing to give a little free advice in exchange for something you do particularly well, whether it's landscaping their yard or drafting a press release—or simply buying them dinner at their favorite restaurant. Check out our resource guide in the back of the book for a list of websites that can help you in your quest. (Oh, and don't be shy about putting things in writing. Just because there's no money changing hands doesn't mean you shouldn't formalize the arrangement. A simple document listing the goods and services you'll be trading, signed by both parties, should be enough to make you both feel solid about your respective commitments.)

❀ Quitting Your Job

If you've been working another job while planning your new business venture, now's the time to give your notice (or at least set a date for your resignation). If your old job has any parallels with your new one, you may want to break it gently to your bosses, particularly if you think they might consider you to be competition. The best policy is to be as up-front as possible, so they can negotiate with you in good faith about how to go forward. (Let's hope you didn't sign a noncompete agreement when you started your job.)

Our advice would be to bring up your big news earlier rather than later, so that everyone has a chance to adjust to it. That said, of course, we don't necessarily advise giving more notice than is legally required; we're just thinking ahead to the networking possibilities. You never know who's going to send you business, and your sales hat goes on NOW!

❀ *By the Books*

There's just one major piece of advice we're going to give you in terms of keeping financial records, which is to err on the side of being a pack rat. Keep every bit of paper pertaining to money that crosses your threshold, either in or out: copies of invoices, receipts, pay stubs (if you have employees), bills, bank and credit card statements, check stubs, and any mail you get from the Internal Revenue Service or your state tax office. It's crucial that you track every cent that crosses your threshold, whether it's coming in or going out—so get in the habit of asking for receipts for all your expenses, *and* keeping records of the money you're pulling in. If you can issue receipts, that's ideal— but for some, a simple pencil-and-paper system (or a spreadsheet) will suffice.

You would also do well to channel your inner accountant and put together some kind of filing system, but essentially the goal here is to take a good look at yourself and decide whether you are the type of person who enjoys meticulous filing, or not. (Be honest—we're not judging you on your answer!) If the answer is "not," now is the time to enlist the services of a good bookkeeper.

Any bookkeeper worth her salt will be able to set you up with some kind of system that makes it easy for you to keep your paper- work in order. One hairstylist friend has twelve months' worth of large manila envelopes, which are dutifully stuffed with receipts, bills, and so on and mailed to the bookkeeper at the end of each month. We, on the other hand, are finance geeks and like to track our own books using spreadsheets, accounting software, and a paper-filing system; at the end of the fiscal year, we email our accounting file to our bookkeeper and drop off the accompanying paperwork for her to sift through.

Bookkeeping is typically a fairly small expense (although the less you do yourself, the more it will cost, obviously), but is one of the best investments you can possibly make. When your finances are in good hands, you can rest better knowing that your butt is covered in the event of a tax audit.

And even if the best you can do is to throw everything in a box and let the bookkeeper make sense of it every couple of months, you'll be glad you took on some help when it comes time to figure out why you're struggling to make rent every month—or where that big chunk of cash in the bank came from. (We hope it's the latter scenario!)

TIME SHEETS

If your work is based on an hourly rate, or if you have staff, there is one more piece of paperwork we insist you do, and that is time sheets. This can be as simple as tracking time in your day planner, but you need a system that allows you to calculate the total time spent on any given project—and it must be accurate. (In fact, depending on your location, you may be required by law to keep time sheets if you bill by the hour.)

Even (in fact, especially) if you quote your work on a fixed-cost basis, you need to have an internal method of measuring how accurate your quotes are. But even if you're a chiropractor working in fifteen-minute intervals, it might be useful to keep track of the clients who routinely keep you waiting, or take up more than their share of your time, so that you can assess the cost of keeping them on.

A Note on Accounting Software

These days there's some pretty fabulous accounting software out there, and lots of those books that purport to instruct "dummies" on how to use it. For our money, though, the best approach to setting up your finances on your computer is to rope in a bookkeeper to help you select, install, and set up the software, and train you on how to use it. What takes a professional a couple of hours will likely take you much, much longer, and a bookkeeper will be able to give you all kinds of time-saving advice and pointers specific to your line of business.

You may not need to take this step for a couple of years—we were in business four years before taking the plunge—but if you're in any kind of product-based or retail business, it will serve you well to go this route, as you'll be able to generate reports on your best-selling product lines, your profitability, and your cash flow with the click of a mouse. Creating those reports manually could take hours, even days—and if you know what your hourly rate is, a quick calculation will tell you whether you're better off investing time or money.

❧ Getting Ready to Open

If you aren't in the working-from-home camp, you'll have some work ahead of you to furnish and decorate your space. Here's another opportunity for those friends of yours to gather round and contribute some sweat equity: Put together a painting party, or put out a call for donations of old chairs. Maybe one of your buddies is a thrift store hound, with an eye for a good deal: Put her in charge of sourcing office furniture. Or perhaps you know someone with a well-equipped workshop who can lend you a sander and a decent saw to help you with your front desk project. Don't be afraid to ask for help here—although it may seem like a huge favor to you, many people are delighted to be asked to pitch in on making a friend's dream come true. (Just maybe be prepared to go without birthday presents for a while.)

When the paint's on the walls, the furniture's in place, and your license is up on the wall, it's time to pause and celebrate. Get yourself some good food and refreshing liquids, invite those helpful friends over, and break in the new space with a rousing party. You've come a long way from the days of wishing and dreaming, and you're well on your way to making a living doing what you love! That's cause for merriment if there ever was one.

MARKETING

MARKETING
Introduction

Is THERE ANYTHING WORSE than being stuck with that guy at the party who can't stop yammering about how successful he is? We all know people who like nothing better than talking about their own greatness. For most of us, it's a pretty off-putting quality—and it's natural to want to avoid being that person. Add to that the fact that most women in our culture are raised with the idea that it's unseemly to take up too much space (physically or otherwise), and you end up feeling like it's a bad thing if you *ever* bring up your own achievements. When was the last time you took full credit for one of your accomplishments? (If it was recently, then rock on, sister! And you can skip this pep talk section and move on to the next page.)

Really think about this. When you work hard for something and pull it off, how do you react? Do you:

- Tell yourself, "Well, it's about time—I really should have gotten around to this sooner"?

- Take about a second to celebrate, and then plunge straight into the next challenge?

- Play it down—you don't want to make anyone else feel inse-cure or less successful?

- Tell your friends about it, but make sure they know it was a team effort—because you know, if it hadn't been for persons

A, B, and C, you'd never have had the courage/skills/emotional support you needed?

• Downplay it when your friends and family boast about you— after all, you're not the first person in history to do something well, and you wish they'd stop going on about it?

We've all been there—it's hard to just simply sit there and bask in your own glory. It feels uncomfortable, and kind of scary. What if everyone finds out you're not so great after all? What if they think you're full of yourself? What if suddenly no one wants to get stuck with you at the party?

Well, here's the thing: Of course you don't want to go overboard and end up like that blowhard no one wants to get trapped in the bathroom lineup with, but **if you don't take credit for your own achievements, chances are that either someone else will, or nobody will notice.** And in business, neither of those scenarios is acceptable.

So where does that leave us? **In marketing territory.**

Our deepest fear is not that we are inadequate. Our deepest fear is that we are powerful beyond measure. It is our light, not our darkness that most frightens us. We ask ourselves, "Who am I to be brilliant, gorgeous, talented and fabulous?" Actually, who are you not to be? Your playing small does not serve the world. There is nothing enlightened about shrinking so that other people will not feel insecure around you. And, as we let our light shine, we unconsciously give other people permission to do the same. As we are liberated from our own fear, our presence automatically liberates others.

While New Age author Marianne Williamson may not exactly consider herself the muse of DIY marketing, girl-style, the preceding excerpt from her book A Return to Love contains some sage advice when it comes to helping some of us gals get over qualms about being our own cheerleaders.

❀ *Selling Your Soul*

Maybe rising to the occasion and selling yourself isn't your stumbling point. Perhaps you are perfectly comfortable talking about your success, but you've read *No Logo,* still pick up the odd issue of *Adbusters,* or maybe, like Emira, even have a past (or present) as a media activist. If you are by nature or politics skeptical of advertising, how do you begin to think about selling your own wares without feeling like you need to compromise your beliefs?

So here's the thing about all that: Unless you plan to be the next big thing in running shoes (in which case you may want to pick up another book or two), marketing doesn't have to be a major endeavor designed to sell a big image in order to distract your buyers from a crappy product. It's not like you are going to set out to market your business in ways that make people feel inadequate so they buy more stuff, that insult people's intelligence, or that degrade parts of the population—and if that *is* your plan, again, you'll want a different book. This is your business now, and we encourage you to rewrite those rules. In order for your marketing to be effective, it has to be developed and used in ways that resonate with the image you want to project.

Take all those fabulous owners of women-positive sex shops, for example (we're thinking Good Vibrations, Babeland, Come As You Are, and others like them): They've been using cheeky, fun, celebratory images of women to sell their quality sex toys for decades now. And in the process they've had a chance to flip the whole women-as-sex-objects thing on its head. If it works for them, why not take a similar approach to your marketing endeavors, and see if you can subvert the dominant paradigm while you promote your wares?

When you think about menstruation, do you think "fun"? Probably not. But our successful pals Madeleine and Suzanne at Lunapads International Products would like it if you did. Tired of images of shame, inconvenience, and that wacky blue liquid being used to sell menstrual products, they set out to work with a designer to come up with ads that would be about finding the joy in being a healthy chick with her period. One of their marketing taglines— "It's still your period: Now it's fun"—reminds women that they're not promising a miracle cure, just offering them an alternative that isn't about making them feel bad for who they are.

So then, you ask, what's going to work for you? Good question.

❀ Definitions

First off, here's how we're going to define marketing for the purposes of this book. This is not the definition of marketing you'll find in business textbooks, but that's the point, right? **Marketing is everything you do that promotes your business,** from producing materials (like business cards, letterheads, a website, brochures, and catalog), to paying for an ad, to showing up at the city's hottest gallery opening sporting a necklace from your stunning new spring line. Anything that represents your business to the world, and that has as its goal bringing positive attention to your business, is marketing.

A lot of us think of some of this stuff—PR, for instance—as the sole domain of the megacorps of the world. The other day we were talking to a friend about public relations, and her reaction was "Wow, that'd have to be the worst job—always apologizing for big businesses' environmental disasters and stuff." That *is* one type of PR work (it's called "crisis PR"), but in reality, PR companies come in all shapes and sizes, just like any other industry—and many organizations do their own PR, too. PR for your company could consist of keeping in touch with a few fashion journalists, if you're making shoulder bags, or throwing an open house and inviting the best-connected folks you know, if you're in retail. (Tip: Always include the best hairstylists in town—they know ridiculous numbers of people!)

The key here is that for every tactic the megacorps use, there may be a parallel one that will work for you—without making you feel icky in the process. It's just a matter of finding an approach that feels right to you, and that allows you to feel comfortable while you're showing off your brilliance to the universe.

❧ *To Market, to Market*

The chapters that follow in this section are all about getting you and your goods out to the world so that you can make your first and subsequent sales. We've spent countless hours with other small business owners like you, talking about what marketing tips and tricks they have picked up along the way, and what they wish they had known before they started. These are some of the craftiest, slyest, and smartest women we know in the business, and we're so happy that they've shared their infinite wisdom with us.

This section is going to take you all the way from figuring out who your audience is (Chapter 5) through finding ways to reach out to them that work for you (Chapters 6–9). We'll be working from six basic marketing principles, which you're welcome to copy out, stick on some poster board, and use as your guiding light as you sell your soul (just kidding).

❋ *The super-important, priceless principles of marketing, according to us*

(feel free to cut out and put on your fridge):

1. It's all about telling the world that you exist—and just how fabulous you are.

2. Would you talk to your mother like that? Speak to your target market with an appropriate voice. (It may not be the same one you'd use to speak to everyone else.)

3. Don't try to please everyone. Forget about the customers you don't want. In fact, you may want a plan to get rid of them!

4. One size never fits all: Not every marketing technique is appropriate for every business.

5. Make your customers feel like they're a part of something (a.k.a. brand your business).

6. Once they know your name, don't let them forget it. Make sure your target market knows when you've done something new and/or noteworthy.

Chapter 5

Addressing Your Audience

So: YOU KNOW WHAT YOUR business is about, right? You've laid out your goals and your mission statement back in Chapters 1 and 2, and it's time to get on to the fun stuff like making killer business cards and cute stationery, right? Whoa, slow down there, *chica*. Before you get all hot to trot about sending your press releases and buying up ad space, you need to figure out what language you are going to use to speak to your new groupies. And while we do mean language in the literal sense—if your plan is to set up shop in delightful Montreal, you'd better *parlez français, mademoiselle!*—we also mean the tone and voice you'll use to communicate with your soon-to-be-paying customers.

It's critical that you get really clear about what you are going to say to your audience and how you are going to say it *before* you actually start developing marketing materials and executing your marketing plan; otherwise your chances of being effective are slim to nil. People out there—the people who will eventually pay you money in exchange for your goods and services—are increasingly bombarded with marketing messages everywhere they go, and you need to make sure that the contact you have with them—everything from your store sign to a billboard on the highway (if you're really going big)—will catch their attention and give them the information they need to notice and remember you.

Equally important in determining how to address your audience is figuring out who is *not* your audience. Now, you don't need to get too hung up on this—likely there are big sections of the population that are by default not going to fall under your spell—but thinking about some of the grayer areas will help you to focus your message and take some risks to really grab the audience you want.

> ▶ Bring Your Own Bag makes reusable cloth tote bags that feature striking designs. The company's environmental focus—both in the creation of the bags, which are locally manufactured and available in organic cotton, and in the overall concept of reducing plastic bag consumption—has made them a favorite of "green" consumers. Meanwhile, though, their memorable, screen-printed graphics attract the attention of style hounds. As such, BYOB's marketing has to appeal to both fashionistas and environmentalists (as well as those who fall somewhere in between).

Determining how you'll talk to your audience and what you'll say to them when you've finally earned their attention is about more than just ensuring you don't offend them; it's also about making sure the right people are listening.

We touched on the importance of specializing in Chapter 2, and when it comes to marketing, it's important that you know exactly whom you want to talk to and what you want them to know before you set out to execute your marketing plan. Equally important is figuring out who your market *isn't,* and making sure you don't spend too much time trying to appease them at the expense of really connecting with the audience you want.

❈ Would You Talk to Your Mother Like That?

Get out that list of who your audience is (and isn't), and those target market profiles we had you write, and start to get into the mind of your customers. Are they looking to be shocked by you? Titillated? Or is the most important thing to them going to be your superlative level of professionalism? While you may describe your business one way to your family at the reunion, your clientele probably expects you to talk to them in a slightly different voice. To wit: "Hey, Aunt Marsha, remember how you taught me how to crochet all those years ago? Now I've got a store where I sell all kinds of hand-crocheted accessories." Compare that to "Come check out our super-sassy crocheted bikinis and hot pants in this season's most enticing colors!" Each has its place, but they're not quite interchangeable. Your customers want to know more about you than the nuts and bolts of what you've got on offer; they want to get a sense of just what to expect from you when they purchase your products/services.

> ► If you sell your goods wholesale, a big part of your marketing plan will involve finding new retailers to sell your wares—and if you're lucky, those retailers will take care of a lot of your direct-to-customer marketing for you (whether through advertising or by talking up your products to customers in the store). But here's something you may not have thought of: If you can get your foot in the door with the trendsetting shops, others may well follow of their own accord. According to Teri Dimalanta, once she got a couple of stores to carry Giddy Giddy hair clips, it wasn't long before she heard from those stores' competitors and was filling orders. The reason? The other stores make a habit of "shopping the competition" to keep on top of new product lines. So Teri recommends doing your research to find the "vanguards"—the shops that are high-profile, or that have a reputation for stocking their shelves with unusual items—and approaching them first.

The other day our pal Signy, a highly accomplished business coach who works primarily with successful businesswomen, called us up to ask if she could really describe her services as "a kick in the pants" on her website. She was, not too surprisingly, questioning whether she could really afford to take the risk of being that cheeky and provocative with people who may very well never have met her—and who have simply stopped by her website to learn a little bit more about her. Now although we're generally nice gals (and so is Signy), and we can't really imagine telling Aunt Lena we've got a friend who would like to kick her in the pants, it *does* come pretty close to how we would describe Signy's services to people we really think would benefit from them.

And here's where principle numero three of our marketing credo comes into play: Don't always try to please everyone. Why? You'll end up not catching anyone's eyes or ears. It's true: The language you use to communicate with your customers may in fact repel others out there . . . and so long as you're getting the right tone with the right people, that's perfectly all right. Being really clear about your marketing messages will help bring you the kinds of customers you want, and help keep the others away. In Signy's case, she's ready to take a risk with her marketing. She has an established practice and wants new clients to be women who will challenge her to work in a full-force kind of environment, so she's okay with discouraging the ones who don't have the stomach for that from picking up the phone.

Figuring out what voice you want to use to speak to your customers can be challenging. At the risk of sounding like one of those crazy guys at the back of the bus, it's worth getting inside the minds of your various target market profiles and trying to evaluate how they would react to some different messaging approaches. Will Liz, the ace bike courier, who has no time for crap, really care about how many pockets are in your reinforced waterproof messenger bags? Or does she just want to see a photo of a girl like her, soaked from a day on the job wearing that bag and staring down the camera? Now, that may not mean ditching the product description altogether, because Theresa, the student whom you've also identified as your customer, is going to want to know that her laptop and day planner are going to fit in those snug compartments, but you're going to have to do your best to address both of them if you want them to respond with enthusiasm.

❧ *Split the Difference*

What if your target markets don't always agree? Maybe Liz wants to see that bag on a totally athletic chick with tattoos, while Theresa is more into something a bit softer around the edges. Often you can straddle the line between the two and come up with something that the majority of your target market will respond to. Sometimes you can't, though, and that may be okay, too. Depending on what venue you're sending your message out to, you can change the content and even the look of it a bit to suit the people you're talking to. Let's take the messenger bag as an example.

If you're buying an ad in a magazine for urban cyclists, your ad may talk exclusively about the waterproof construction, comfy strap, and reflective safety tape on the edging. And you may accompany that with a photo of a girl wearing the bag, with a bike in the background. But then, when the cool fashion column writer calls and wants to write a story about those bags that seem to be popping up everywhere, you may instead focus on the many colors they come in, different sizes that are available, and multiple uses that the bags have been put to. The trick here is that you aren't spinning contradictory fictions to each audience—after all, that cyclist may still read the fashion column— you're just highlighting different aspects of your product or service based on who you're talking to.

Same goes for Signy. While it may be A-okay for her to describe her services in cheeky language on her own website, when she's writing her bio for a coaching article she's submitting to a publication read by other coaches, she may want to tone it down a bit and focus instead on her successful track record, list of satisfied clients, and accreditation.

You can always focus your message for different audiences, especially when you know that you have a chance to capture different types of people's attention. Just remember, you are still putting your message out in the public sphere, so don't do things that you think will totally alienate an important segment of your audience—simply use the opportunity to specialize.

❀ Getting Focused

Before a big megacorp releases a product into the market, they do some test runs with real live people they've identified as representative of their audience. If you've ever been hard up for cash, you may have even attended one of these sessions, where you get to wax poetic about the new font on the paper towel packaging, or let them know if the new, low-cal version of their carbonated beverage tastes as good as the full-sugar version. And while you likely don't have the cash to pay a bunch of perfect strangers $50 a head to sit in a room and talk about your new ad, packaging design, or product, this is another perfect time to wrangle up some friends and get their input. So crack out the cookies (or cocktails, depending on how long you want them to stay focused) and call up some pals.

This process can be as formal or informal as you like. It could even just be calling up a friend one evening and running your website copy by them—as Signy did—or asking the girl who runs the store next door what she thinks of your new packaging mock-up. But if you are making a fairly major—and somewhat irreversible—decision, you may want to put some time into this, get some people together, and really pay attention to the feedback they give you.

What to do if your friends and family aren't your target audience? Good question. While you may not have the cash on hand to pay the kinds of folks who are, you may be able to actually make some strategic use of existing or potential customers here—and possibly drum up business on the side. You can offer discounts or giveaways to people who are the right audience and are willing to participate. If you've already got a business up and running to some degree, try asking your existing customers if they'd like to give you some feedback.

> ► While in-person focus groups are effective, there are online options as well. Many companies that design their own products have benefited from using their blogs to gather input on prospective designs before putting them into production. You can set up a blog for free (see the Resource Guide for more information), and if you've got the kind of business where gathering customer input is valuable, all it takes is a few minutes of your time to post a question (and possibly an accompanying picture or two). Open it up to comments, and see what your customers have to say!

❋ The Elevator Speech

Creating your "elevator speech" is one of those things that traditional business books will tell you are really important before you go out and start acting like a businessperson in the real world. And frankly, the term—and the image it conjures up of people in suits in an elevator exchanging business cards and pithy descriptions about their work—has always kind of made us recoil from this marketing staple, but without some version of it you'll find yourself at a loss for words at all the wrong moments. So while you may never use your speech in a fancy office building elevator, you will want to have something memorable and focused to say the next time someone asks you what you do for a living—especially if that someone is a potential customer/client.

Your sound bite about your business should be a logical extension of your mission statement, so dig up your work from Chapter 2; you can use it to supply you with key words and phrases. Of course, your elevator speech is not actually something you need to memorize and repeat, all cyborglike, any time anyone asks you what you do—and as with marketing to different audiences, it may shift a bit depending on who you're talking to. But you need to have something at the ready, and it should be both succinct and descriptive, giving the person on the other end of it enough information that they really know what it is you do after they excuse themselves and head back to the cheese plate.

In coming up with your description, try to keep it short. This is important, and ultimately it is one of the big benefits to doing this kind of prep work. If you don't have something at the ready, then you're likely to answer the "so what do you do?" question with a long-winded description of all the little things you do in a day, and why they're interesting (to you).

When we first started out, and hadn't really got clear on how to answer that question—even though we had a tagline, mission statement, and clear set of goals—we would typically give a rambling answer that went something like this: "Oh yeah, well, we have a small business and we build websites. Yeah, I know, everyone builds websites these days, right? Yeah. So we mainly focus on not-for-profit and arts groups, and sometimes activists too. Oh! And, we really like working with women, but we don't only work with women or anything, except that we find we often do work with them. And oh yeah, we like working with women-owned businesses. And sometimes we do real estate work, but we're not really looking to expand in that direction. But yeah, we've done some of that. Oh, what's that? No, we don't do print work. Just web work. Yeah. Websites. We build websites."

That's not so helpful, is it? You get a sense of what we do, but not in anything resembling a clear or memorable format, and you don't really get a sense of the company at all, except to know that it is a small business run by two women who do all kinds of websites and not print work. Here's the "elevator speech" version: "We specialize in building websites for not-for-profits, arts groups, and women-owned business. We've worked on all kinds of projects, locally and internationally, but are mainly focusing on large, content-heavy websites now." We then go on to list projects we've done that may be of interest to the person we're talking to, particularly if we think they're likely to have seen them. Which is not to say that we've become fantastically eloquent party conversationalists who never use "um" or "huh" in a sentence, simply that we've got the first bit of that answer ready to go—so we've got a chance to warm up and start to figure out just what that stranger whose hand we just shook actually wants to know about our business.

Keep in mind, this little speech is going to change over the years. We now often let people know that we've been in business for eight years when we're giving them the rundown, because in our business that's an excellent track record and lets them know that we're here to stay. We also added in the "large projects" bit a couple of years ago, as that certainly wasn't true when we started out, but a few years into things we found ourselves frustrated that people seemed to perceive the fact that we were a two-person shop as limiting us to taking on small projects only, and we knew different.

So what's your elevator speech going to look like? It only has to be a few sentences long, and it should paint a picture of your business at its absolute best. You want to project the positive here, and let people see your vision, not all the everyday bits and pieces that make it happen. If you have a physical location, make sure you let people know where it is. Sometimes it can be helpful to let them know how you're different from what they might be expecting; tell them why your business is particularly memorable. And if you really want to go for the hard sell, maybe let them know how much they could benefit from your products or services—but be careful with this one, as you need to be genuine here and not too pushy. Don't try to sell your hair services to a bald guy, but do make people feel like they're welcome to find out more and perhaps stop by sometime.

❋ *No More Little Ms. Nice Girl*

Have you got the message yet? While you're definitely looking to make an impression on the masses when it comes to marketing your business, you're not running for class president. You don't need to straddle the line between pleasing the chess club and the jocks; it's time to pick a side. Make your choice, and make sure the people who are going to support you (and buy your stuff) understand why you're a good fit for them.

If you've picked up one piece of wisdom in this chapter, we hope it's that it's okay not to be all things to all people—so long as you're speaking (and listening) to the people who matter most: your target audience. All the marketing, PR, and networking in the world will only get you so far if you're not crystal clear about it is you most want to reach. So, now that we've got that under our belts, we can move on to sorting out what kind of marketing materials you need (and how they should look), as well as the basics of advertising and promotions, public relations, and face-to-face networking.

Just remember, as we dive into the next few chapters: If you're feeling lost, pull out those target market personas and ask yourself what they want to see and hear. They'll keep you on track until you've got real live customers to give you feedback in person.

Chapter 6
Developing Marketing Materials

❀ *Find Your Look*

FINALLY: THE FUN STUFF. After all the lists we've had you make and numbers you've been crunching, when you get to the point of developing the face of your company, it's playtime.

First, dig out those exercises you did in Chapter 2 and the work you did on your competitors and target market in Chapter 5. Have a quick read through your target market profiles again and put yourself in the mind of your new customers as you start to think about how you are going to represent your business. Now you can embark on the process of designing your business cards, stationery, brochure, catalog, signage, and/or website—all the stuff you can hand out, distribute, and show to potential clients that will make them understand who you are.

Before you start panicking about the length of that list, remember Principle #4: One size never fits all, and not every marketing technique is appropriate for every business. When it comes to your materials, you may not need every little thing on offer, especially if you're just getting started. If your business is primarily web based, you probably don't need to spend money on a fancy stationery package, and a brochure certainly isn't going to do you much good. On the other hand, if you're setting up a small, specialized retail shop aimed at local buyers, a website may not serve you as well as materials targeted toward more personalized and local contact.

What you do need is a prioritized list of the swag you are going to produce. To figure that out, ask yourself the following questions:

How are people going to connect with me? In person, over the phone, or online? Depending on what your answer is, focus your efforts where you're going to get the most bang for your buck. For example, if you're going to run a web-based business, don't cheap out on your website, and maybe cool it a bit on the four-color stationery package.

How important are fancy design and aesthetics to my target market? If you're going for the waste-not-want-not enviro crowd, then you're going to design a very different business card than if you're looking to run with fashion-forward hipsters.

What are my competitors doing? If the competition isn't using brochures, there's probably a good reason. Do your homework and see what the norm is in your industry. That said, don't discount the possibility that you may have thought of something they're overlooking; you are, after all, out there to blow them all away, right?

With the answers to the above questions, you should be able to come up with a prioritized list of what kinds of marketing materials you should be spending your precious start-up pennies on, and what stuff can wait until you've got some cash flowing through the business.

All done? Got your prioritized list? Okay, now hang on to it for a few minutes while we take a quick detour to logo land.

> As designers, we often see people making decisions about the public face of their company/organization based solely on their personal taste, without considering who their audience is. Of course you need to like your logo, cards, etc.—but you can't ever forget about how your customers are going to react.

❋ *Leggo My Logo*

A prerequisite for nearly every piece of the marketing materials in your list is a logo. If you don't already happen to be a graphic design genius, coming up with a logo for your business can feel like a daunting task, but that's why there are graphic designers, silly!

If you can't afford to hire a designer (and don't know any who could be persuaded to work in exchange for your killer homemade cookies), you have a few options open to you:

- If your business can handle it, you could draw or design your own. (This would work best for DIY-style businesses, or if, say, you're setting up a graphic design business.)

- Pick your favorite font, type in your business name, and voilà! Logo. (Especially good for businesses where a graphic identity is less important—like a consultancy.)

- Put up a flyer at your local art and design college and see if you can find young designers who want to expand their portfolio.

- Assuming you can pay (even a little bit) for a professionally designed logo, we highly recommend it. (And we're not just saying that because we're designers.) A designer can provide you with much-needed advice and expertise, from choosing colors to making sure your fonts are legible at the small sizes business cards require. They're also invaluable in terms of working with the printers to ensure that your stuff comes out looking the way you expected it to. In the long run, if you can afford it, you'll probably avoid more headaches and unforeseen costs by hiring a professional.

A few tips if you're looking for a logo designer:

- Ask to see their portfolio of logo (sometimes called "identity") work. Make sure they have lots of experience and that you like their work.

- Check references. They should have a long list of happy clients you can call to see how they are to work with.

- Trust your gut. This is a collaborative process, and you want to be sure you're going to feel comfortable.

- Ask to see how their work looks in black and white as well as color. Your logo will need to look just as strong when it's in a newspaper or on a one-color poster as it does in glorious full color.

Once you've got your designer (even if it's you), you'll want to develop a few concepts and run them by a team of highly trusted advisors—here's where you rope in those willing friends and guinea pigs. Getting second, third, and fifteenth opinions is always a great idea before you decide on something, but remember to always take people's feedback with a grain of salt. If your friend who has hopped on that whole '80s revival thing and is wearing stirrup pants as fashion tries to insist that bubble letters are really the next big thing in typography, you may want to smile, thank her, and move on. Getting an outside opinion is useful in many ways (like double-checking whether the name is legible or the design is totally unidentifiable). So once you have narrowed it down to the top candidates, gather your panel of trusted advisors and get ready for some feedback.

If you're totally new to this, here are a few guidelines for judging a good logo:

- Don't get too hung up on it. Like your business name, it needs to be something you can stand to look at for a long time to come, but you can always change it, as long as you can also afford to change your marketing materials. There's no need to compete with the famous swoosh just yet.

- Try to set yourself apart so that you can develop brand recognition, but a logo is only going to do so much for you—your other marketing materials, and indeed the rest of your business plan, will do the rest.

- Be wary of trends. That doesn't mean you need to be dull or painfully predictable, but try to think about longevity when

picking your logo. If there is a font or color that you are seeing absolutely everywhere you look lately and that you totally
adore—pick another. Chances are it is a look that will seem
dated in a matter of months.

There are two basic directions you can take with logos: Staid and
Safe, and Out on a Limb. The former has its advantages—people usually "get it" right away, and if your target market is conservative, this
is probably where you want to be. Going out on a limb could mean
anything from using a bold and unusual signature color—we've had
a lot of success using pink, which in the technology world is pretty
unusual—to crafting an icon that's really obscure, which may appeal
to customers who want to feel like they're part of an exclusive, special group. Choose your style based on your target market and on
how important it is for you to make waves, visually speaking, with
your business.

❀ *Now Back to Our Regularly Scheduled Programming . . .*

Now, where were we? Ah, yes: developing your marketing materials.
Pick up that prioritized list you made a couple of pages ago; we're
going to walk you through each item in turn and how to go about
getting the most bang for your buck out of the ones you choose.

Business Cards: Although these are often at the top of people's
minds when they start a new business, they usually aren't the most
creative things around. They're small, albeit functional, promotional
items, and let's face it—very few people are going to pore over them
for longer than a second or two. The main reason you need them is so
that you can quickly and efficiently give people your contact information. So make sure that's the focus, and that your phone number,
email address, and any other salient details are prominent and legible.
If you're in a design-oriented industry, try printing on interesting card

stock, or having your cards cut to unusual dimensions or shapes for added visual impact—but don't go too crazy; this isn't where you want to spend all your time and energy.

Money-saving tip: For cheap but pretty cards, visit your local print shop and ask the experts behind the counter for suggestions. You can save money by choosing digital printing rather than conventional printing, and/or by opting for black ink (perhaps on nicely colored and/or textured card stock), rather than full color.

Stationery: Most of us can make do with a couple of Word templates and a decent printer, but if your business involves a lot of mailing, custom-printed stationery may be a good investment. If shipping your products is one of the primary ways you interact with your clients, consider having your most popular forms (e.g., invoices, order forms, and so on) and mailing labels designed by a professional for an extra-slick look. (A designer can often help with making complex forms user-friendly, too.) Consultants and other people whose businesses entail a lot of paper correspondence may need professional-looking letterhead. Whatever the case, you're going to want something easy to use and highly functional—this isn't the place for flights of fancy, unless that's what your brand is all about.

If you aren't absolutely sure your business has found a permanent (or at least semipermanent) home, hold off on getting your address printed on your stationery. Stick with the stuff you can take with you, like your phone number, website, and email address. That way, you won't have to pay to have everything reprinted when you move across town (or down the hall).

Letterhead designs should always include two page designs—one for the cover page of any letter, and another for the second page. The second page should be much simpler (even a blank page, in the same paper stock as the cover, will do)—it doesn't need all the flash of the cover, since it will be tucked in behind.

Brochures: Let's face it—the world is full of boring, three-panel brochures that no one is compelled to pick up. If you've decided that a brochure is important to your business, you may want to consider doing it a little differently. Perhaps a two-sided, four-by-five-inch card would do the trick, or a wee, stapled booklet. Your logo designer may have some ideas for you here. If a three-panel brochure is in the cards for you, make it stand out by making sure it speaks clearly to your target market, and choosing your materials carefully; good paper can make all the difference in the world.

Be sure to ask for help when you're writing. Bring in outside readers to give you a fresh perspective—and some spell-checking!

Don't be afraid to use your word processor's templates if you can—they make a great starting point for young businesses, and they'll save you money if you can't afford to have your brochure professionally designed.

Catalogs: Those of you in the market for a catalog have potentially the most expensive marketing piece in the bunch—but don't let that stop you if it's really what you need. Depending on the extent of your product line, your major investment here is probably going to be getting high-quality photos taken. (In some cases, custom illustration work could also be appropriate—and unusual enough to help you stand out from the crowd. But remember that most customers will probably want to see your products "in the flesh"—i.e., in photos—before they buy.) We highly recommend getting professional photos done, as they'll stand you in good stead in other places, too (like your brochure, website, packaging, and press kits), and as we all know from seeing those pretty magazine ads, a top-notch photograph can make pretty nearly anything look irresistible.

Your goal here is to sell your product—so make sure the ordering information is prominent and crystal clear.

There are graphic designers out there who specialize in catalog work. If your catalog is going to be your most important marketing tool, it may be worthwhile talking to a specialist. They shouldn't cost more than anyone else; they've just carved out a niche and are extra-good at catalog work.

Websites: Okay, bear with us—we do this for a living, so we may go on a bit. Once again, we're going to recommend you work with a professional if you can afford it, because a good web designer will be able to help you sort out the complexities of domain names, hosting, design, and maintenance. (On the other hand, there are a lot of charlatans in this business, too, who take advantage of their clients and overcharge them for mediocre work. Don't allow yourself to be oversold by a zealous designer who insists that your small retail store *needs* an e-commerce system that rivals Amazon's.) That said, if you're a computer-savvy person willing to put in some elbow grease, a website is arguably one of the easiest marketing tools for you to create on your own—especially if it's a straightforward one.

Remember, on the web, content is queen, so the key to keeping people coming back to your site is to provide them with good stuff to read and/or look at—make sure you're ready to make regular updates to your site. Also, don't overlook the huge potential you've got in your website visitors; most businesses can benefit from having an email newsletter that visitors can sign up for, even if the newsletter consists of quarterly sale notices or rehashed press releases. This is one of the cheapest and most effective marketing tools available, if you use it well. (See Chapter 7 for more on email marketing.)

A few key points to remember when developing your website:

Good print designers are not always good web designers. Whoever you talk to about doing your site, ask to see a portfolio of web-specific work. (This should be an online portfolio so you can actually check out how the sites work.)

If your business name isn't available in its original form as a domain name, try appending a descriptive word after it. (For example, when Romp, a Brooklyn store that sells kids' toys, furniture, and more, went to purchase a domain name, they found that www.romp.com wasn't available, but www.rompbklyn.com was—*et voilà!* A nice, short, and descriptive domain name.)

Think of your website as an extension of your business; you should be getting a measurable return on investment. In other words, if you're going to put, say, $3,000 into your site, you should feel confident that you'll get your money's worth, whether in sales, business leads, or simple exposure. Every business has its own goals for online marketing; make sure yours are clearly defined so your designer (even if that's you) can work toward getting measurable results (e.g., 10 percent of total sales online, an average of a thousand unique visitors a month, or just fewer phone calls to your office for answers to frequently asked questions).

Packaging: If you're in the product development (or retail) business, packaging is the signature outfit for your treasured goods. It can be tempting to break the bank here, because who doesn't want their babies to look their best? But remember that simplicity is a look, too—and can be quite an effective one. A nice, brown paper bag with a sticker closure can be just as effective as a big striped one with a nifty handle. As with all marketing materials, you'll want to make sure your packaging reflects your target market, so that you aren't putting your funky guitar straps into overly girly boxes, or glittery lip gloss into boring-o-rama tubes. In the end, though, your product is the thing you need to sell—not the thing it comes in. Aim to find a balance by putting together a package that adds to but doesn't overwhelm the product.

For products that require their own packaging, such as liquids (jars/bottles), cosmetics (boxes, tubes, pots, etc.), foodstuffs, and so on, there's a whole world of packaging options out there—but you'll probably find it's most affordable to purchase a package in a common shape (say, a typical shampoo bottle), and have stickers made that reflect your brand. The advantage to using stickers is that it's way easier to print up new stickers than it is to develop a whole new line of preprinted bottles.

> *If you are developing a product or line for distribution, you are really best to work with a professional for your packaging design. Find a graphic designer who has experience in this area, and when you are first meeting, test out how creative the designer is at problem solving and sourcing cheap packaging. A little ingenuity here may save you a lot in the long run as you are looking at ordering hundreds or thousands of these suckers.*

Retailers shouldn't be afraid to use boring old paper or plastic bags (unless your target market is really upscale) and personalize them a bit.

► When Jenny Hart started Sublime Stitching, she had a generic package she used for all her patterns—envelopes that she got printed with all her info, with the exception of the pattern style. To save money on printing costs, she had a rubber stamp for each pattern, and as she packaged her patterns, she would stamp every envelope with the relevant image. Cat patterns got a rubber-stamped cat, pirate patterns were stamped with a pirate, and so on. As her business grew, hand-stamping each pattern became impractical, but she has fond memories of that personal touch that grew out of financial necessity.

Signage: If your business relies on foot traffic, you'll need some signs to mark your territory. A sign could take the form of a window graphic, a sandwich board, an awning, or any number of other options. (Vegas-style neon, anyone?) Just make sure they're visible from the sidewalk *and* the street, so that pedestrians and drivers alike can spot you.

> ▶ When one of our favorite dress shops opened their doors a few years ago, they brought the ultrafemme theme of their store out to the sidewalk with a little faux white picket fence and flower box that sat outside the store in place of a conventional sign.

Wee Goodies: We've noticed more and more small businesses producing funky swag that's a far cry from those notepads you get in the mail from realtors. Here are a few ideas for cheap and cheerful items you can produce without breaking the bank—and that people will actually use and enjoy:

- *Stickers:* These little gummy wonders have so many purposes—return-address labels, notebook decorations, paperbag fasteners . . . and they're dirt cheap to produce. You can develop your own using a decent word processor and some office supply store labels, or hire a designer to whip some up for you. They're not necessarily going to give you a huge return on your investment, but it's mighty fun to slap your sticker on an envelope and revel in its beauty.

- *Buttons:* One of our neighborhood shops has a make-it-yourself button machine they happily rent out for short-run button making, and it's used frequently by artists, crafters, activists, and self-promoters of all stripes. If you've got a strong visual identity (and a message that can be conveyed in one square inch or less), buttons are a great way to spread the word about your business. (Not only that, but you can make them in small runs—say, one hundred at a time—and change the design as frequently as you like, making them the perfect marketing tool for the easily bored entrepreneur.)

- *Fridge Magnets:* Okay, these have definitely been abused in the past, but lately we've seen some gorgeous examples that have restored our faith in the power of magnet-ude. A local jeweler we know put together promotional magnets that feature a simple, stunning photograph of her work—that's it. It's up to the fridge's owner to explain further. They're the perfect conversation starter when friends come over to raid the fridge.

❀ *That's a Wrap!*

Your marketing materials are, in many ways, the public face of your company. They create a feeling with which potential and existing customers can identify and want to be associated. Take the same care in developing them that you would in choosing an outfit for a very special occasion, but don't forget that you can always start small and develop your dream website (or catalog, or brochure) once you've got a few sales under your belt.

By now you should have a grasp of your business's look, as well as the voice you'll be using to communicate with your audience. With your message and materials well on their way, the next step is to choose the right medium for spreading the word.

CHAPTER 7
Advertising and Promotions

❈ From Graffiti to Billboards

If you're reading this book, chances are a billboard ad campaign is probably a little bit overboard for your business, but advertising can take many forms. In the next chapter we will be covering one of the cheapest and most effective forms of advertising—word of mouth—but paying for some direct ad exposure can be an important step in your marketing plan as well.

The great thing about advertising is that it gives you a chance to show off your message to the big wide world—or at least the readers of the magazine/paper/etc. in question. The drawback is that getting the attention of those eyeballs is often not cheap. It can also be a bit hard to directly measure the success of your ads—though if no one is buying, you can surmise they aren't working.

These days there are more venues for paid advertising than we ever thought possible—from the more traditional newspaper, magazine, radio, and TV ads to space inside bathroom cubicles and in the back seats of cabs. For many of you, the idea of adding to that public noise may make you break out in hives, but apply some lotion, take a deep breath, and read on.

❧ How Do You Choose the Medium That's Right for You?

As with all of your marketing, you need to spend some time thinking like your target audience. Think about where your customers are likely to hang out, what they read, and where they spend their hard-earned dollars. Then figure out how you can make them notice you in those situations. If you are making a product—anything from hats to lip gloss—you should probably look at advertising in an appropriate magazine or paper. The two things to consider are a) who the audience for the publication is, and b) what kind of reach it has. If you are selling your cupcakes out of a store on the main drag, then you probably don't want to advertise in a national yoga magazine, no matter how many of your customers stop by after a good yoga-thon. Likewise, if you're selling your deconstructed denim skirts online, skip paying for ads in the local lefty weekly; the reach just isn't big enough. (As we'll cover in the next section, though, do try to get that rag to write a story about you.) Take a look at what others in your field are doing, where they're advertising, and see if it makes sense for you as well.

If you choose to go the print advertising route (i.e., advertising in newspapers or magazines), don't be afraid to negotiate; ad rates are usually flexible, and they'll vary depending on how many issues you're willing to commit to, as well as how hard you're willing to bargain. Once you've established a relationship with key advertising venues, you'll have even more bargaining power. One businesswoman we spoke to told us that two of the magazines she's advertised with for years usually increase her rates every year. If they raise them to a point where it's no longer affordable, however, she'll simply call up their ad rep and try to negotiate a better deal—her strongest bargaining chip is the fact she's been a stalwart supporter of the magazines for so long that for them to replace her ad revenue would be a bit of a daunting task.

Once you've decided where to spend your ad dollars (or what neighborhood to blast with posters), you're going to need an ad. All you're getting with advertising is a piece of real estate on a page, screen, or wall of your choice; there are no guarantees that folks are going to pay attention—so you need something eye-catching and memorable to make sure they do. Hiring a graphic designer can often be money well spent, as once you've paid for the ad space you want it to work well—but it can also be pricey. If you think you can come up with something yourself, or you've got a friend to help you, by all means give it a whirl. Be sure to do your research and look into what the other ads yours will be surrounded by tend to look like. Ideally, yours will be of the same or better caliber in terms of its design quality, and will stand out enough to get noticed. Remember to get the design guidelines—things like the print resolution, size specifications, and whether the ad will be in black and white or color—from the publication or media you've bought advertising space from, before anyone gets started.

Paying for ads isn't always an option, or the best answer. Another much more DIY approach to advertising can be to use that public space that is already so cluttered with ads as your own canvas. If you are opening up a new store, or promoting an event, the old paste-and-paper poster route can be a very successful form of advertising. So can stickers or postcards, which can be left in local coffee shops or hangouts—again chosen based on where your target market is likely to be spending their time. When it comes to posters, cards, or flyers, the same rules apply as in advertising placement; you want to stand out and be noticed. Unless you're really going for a low-budget feel, you're probably going to want to use some color, which can bring up the price. But you don't have to go for full-color, high-gloss printing if it's going to break the bank; great things can be achieved with colored paper and a black-and-white photocopier. Then all you have to do is get out there and do the legwork to get your swag in coffee shops and on street corners around town. Depending again on budget and your time, you can actually hire people to poster or do card drop-offs for you in some major towns, but it is also a great way to recruit friends to get in the game and lend you a hand.

In addition to wanting something that looks sharp, you'll want to keep these key points in mind when developing an ad:

Simplicity is a virtue. While you may have all kinds of tricks up your sleeve or goodies in your bag, you don't want to overwhelm people. You've only got their attention for a few moments, so unless abundance is your raison d'être, hone your message so that it's easy to communicate and memorable.

You tease! Ultimately you want people to get in touch with you in some way (come into your store, buy your goods, or call you for work), so make sure your message either intrigues them enough that they want to learn more or gives them a reason to get in touch, like a promotion or special.

Aim for your target. If you're advertising in a niche publication, consider designing an ad specifically for its readers, with an eye to what they might find most interesting about your business. For example, when Cinnamon Cooper decided to advertise her Poise bags in *Bitch* magazine (which discusses pop culture with a feminist bent), she created an ad that focused on a single product in her line: a bag with a pro-choice symbol on the front. Her sales were higher from that ad than from previous attempts that advertised her entire range.

Call me anytime . . . Make sure you include the important contact details: your address, phone number, and/or website location. (Everyone who has ever been involved in event organizing has at some time seen a poster go out into the world missing a vital piece of info—location, time, date, or what-have-you. This happened to a good friend of ours who threw a sing-along *Purple Rain* event as part of a retro club series. While the handful of us who were in the know had a great time belting it out alongside the little purple man, attendance was not what it would have been if the location of the club had made it onto the posters.)

> *If there are magazines that cater to your particular niche, they're often your best bet for advertising. Not only do niche magazines have smaller, more focused circulation, but they also have correspondingly lower ad rates than the supermarket glossies. And frequently, their readership is devoted enough that they pay attention to even the small ads in the "classified" section in the back— a section that in higher-profile magazines will net you very little reader attention.*

❋ Going Viral

Viral marketing—along with "leverage," "solutions provider," and "thinking outside the box"—is one of those business terms that can make your teeth itch if you hear it too many times, but for the savvy small business gal it's actually worth paying attention to. If it isn't obvious, viral marketing refers to the trend whereby ideas spread like viruses (clever, hey?) through society. The goal here is to make your products or services—previously only a dream in your own mind— known to society at large. What you want to do is get your message out to a few key people and then have them spread it further, until there's a general buzz among your potential customers about just how fine your business is.

Of course, these days, one of the easiest ways to spread an idea is by email, and really this trick works for almost all businesses (the exception being those who anticipate a market that is pretty much unwired). What you want to do is develop an email that will be interesting and/or cool enough that people are going to want to send it to all their friends, who will in turn send it to their friends, family, and colleagues. The great thing about email is that it is also pretty cheap. But as with traditional ads, most folks are already faced with pretty full inboxes, so you want to make sure your message is going to stand out from the rest, pique their interest, and drive them to take action.

After email, the next most popular trend in electronic viral marketing is most definitely the blog. Blogs (or weblogs) can come in many forms, ranging from personal diary-like sites on which individuals document their thoughts, opinions, and activities to topical blogs, which can focus on everything from food to movies to Pomeranians. And just as *Vogue* magazine has a much larger reach than *Bitch*, different blogs have various audience sizes. That said, our clients have reported pretty notable spikes in sales when a blogger with a dedicated readership happens to offer a hat tip to their products or services. So, if you know of some influential bloggers out there who attract a readership that you think overlaps with your target audience, don't be afraid to treat them like the press and send them updates or products for review.

In addition to online tactics, you may be able to use some of the more tangible tools you've already developed—stickers, catalogs, or brochures—as your messengers. If you have direct contact with your customers, either in person or by mail, make brochures, stickers, or general swag for your customers to spread around for you.

> When sending out an email about your business, be careful about who you send your initial email out to. Sending it out to folks who don't know you at all or whose permission you don't have amounts to spam—and nobody likes a spammer. So send the message to folks who aren't going to be surprised to receive it, and you'll cultivate a relationship based on trust. That trust will pay off in the long run; a loyal customer is a thousand times more likely to

recommend you to their friends than someone who feels harassed by unsolicited emails.

If you find that your email list is a little on the slim side, see if you can come up with a promotional offer that might entice new people to join. It could be as simple as offering a chance at free or discounted products (or a free consultation, if you're in the service industry) to anyone who signs up—or better yet, to anyone who gets five friends to join!

▶ Hairstylists, massage therapists, and other professionals who rely on word-of-mouth referrals can often pick up new clients simply by sending their existing ones off into the world with a handful of business cards in their wallets. That way, when their new haircut attracts their friends' attention, they can pass them a card—there's no better referral than happy customers who will rave to their pals about your handiwork.

The key to maintaining and building on a viral marketing plan is to build up that initial list, but to do that you need permission. Permission-based marketing basically means what its name implies: getting people's permission to send them your ads, be that by mail, email, or singing telegram. We're all used to signing up for email lists, but if you'd like to build a more tangible customer list, you may also want to collect names and mailing addresses so you can send out revised catalogs, coupons, or postcards to your biggest fans. The great thing about permission-based lists is that they help you maintain and grow your repeat customer list, as these people have literally agreed to be marketed to at some point in the future and so are likely to be receptive to your charms. And repeat customers are very important in the long-term health of any business.

I WANNA BE A BLOG STAR

Using blogs to build your business doesn't just have to be about getting bloggers to notice you and your wares; some businesses have been very successful at getting attention through their own blogs. This works particularly well in two general situations:

1. To help build confidence in your audience that you are an expert.

2. To help build the brand of your business, if your brand is all about you!

One of the biggest benefits to a blog is that it's the perfect way to put a human face to your business—it gives your potential customers a way to see into your world and get to know the person behind the brand. Your blog can help you build that all-important trust relationship with your audience, so they feel like they have a personal connection with you. Especially for small businesses whose public images are all about a personal touch, your personality is your brand, and a business blog is the perfect medium to showcase that personality.

If you can use your blog to tell your target audience just how up-to-date you are on trend watching, and help build your cred as the web's number one stop for designer items at discount prices, then go for it. But if you plan to use your blog to document the ups and downs of your relationship, or to keep logs of your prolific volumes of fan fiction, then you might want to use a pseudonym and keep it a personal, not professional, endeavor.

Don't forget, too, that the commenting feature of many blogs can be put to very good use for your business. Whether you invite comments on product prototypes (as we discussed in Chapter 5) or ask your readers for suggestions on places to sell your wares, you can create a real sense of community by asking for—and responding to—feedback. (Just don't forget that if you're asking your *readers for a favor, you may want to sweeten the pot by offering something in return. Rose Flash, for example, once gave $60 gift certificates to any blog reader whose boutique recommendation resulted in a wholesale order.)*

❀ *Promotions*

So maybe advertising, in the traditional sense, just isn't in your budget this year. Or maybe it is only one piece of your grand plan to take over the world one hand-knit legwarmer at a time. What are your other options? Promoting your products and services can be a little more hands-on than just buying ads in the local weekly, and here's where your networking skills can come into play.

A great way to get some free airtime in the public sphere can be to exchange your goods or services for some word on the street. This can be as simple as an exchange for traditional advertising—see if you've got something a newspaper or magazine is in need of, and do a trade for ad space.

The exchange can also be a bit more elaborate. Create a list of everyone you know and highlight all the people who you think have influence over potential customers. Influence may be measured by some degree of fame (local or otherwise), or may just have to do with a person's position within certain networks. Give free samples of your products or services to those people who you think will get your goods some high profile. If you don't have any high-profile connections, start small. If you've got a friend who you know is a chatty girl about town, give her one of those fetching new bags you've made this season, and be sure to stuff a handful of cards in the pocket.

You can also take on co-promotions with like-minded businesses in ways that you can all benefit from. Put together a gift basket with some other businesses and organize a drawing in a high-traffic location, donate goods to a local charity fund-raising raffle or auction, or if you have a really kindred spirit, see if you can't work out some kind of a trade. Maybe you can give discounts on your yoga clothes to everyone who brings in a juice card from the health food store next door, and you in turn give out coupons for a free shot of wheatgrass with every purchase over $100 from your store. If you've got a website, see if you can tempt other like-minded businesses to trade links (or even ad space) with you. Be creative and strategic; you don't want your offer of free goods to end up as a crumpled piece of paper in someone's pocket—you want it to be compelling enough that it brings you exactly the kind of customers you're looking for.

> ► When we were running our webzine Soapboxgirls as a monthly publication, we exchanged ad space for web design skills with *Bitch* magazine. It was a great trade for both of us, as they didn't have the budget for professional web work and we had absolutely no budget for ads for Soapboxgirls, which was funded solely by our love for the project and the odd late night with vegan cookies.

❋ *Spreading the Word*

We all know that infamous "and she told five friends, and so on, and so on" adage, but when you're flogging your own goods or services, you can't underestimate the power of word of mouth. Of course, word of mouth is also a double-edged sword, and you need to be sure that it is working for and not against you.

In our own industry, word of mouth has been the key to our success. If there is one thing the West Coast has no shortage of, it's website designers—and coffee shops, and yoga studios, and film people—but we digress. We quickly assessed that advertising in the traditional sense was not for us. Even the most innovative print ad would do little to bring us clients that would be a good fit for our services, and online advertising could never be targeted enough—after all, no one decides to spend thousands of dollars on design services based on a banner ad. So really, word of mouth has been our biggest sales agent.

Not only is word of mouth cheap—all it costs you is good ongoing customer service—it's also a great way to get targeted customers, as your existing customers are likely to tell folks just like them all about how impressed they were with your pink coquette underpants with the frilly lace bottoms, and how useful they will be for their own next burlesque number.

The other bonus of word of mouth over traditional advertising is that it doesn't really have an expiration date. If people receive great service or a fabulous product from you, they'll keep talking about it—sometimes for years—whereas a traditional ad is only good as long as you pay for it. After all, how many times have you stopped someone on the street and asked them where they got that fabulous pair of electric blue clogs, only to have them answer that they bought them from some obscure boutique four years ago? Now, that boutique may not be able to sell you those exact shoes anymore, but chances are you'll be poking your nose in there, next time you're in the hood. Likewise, for our own business, some of our biggest projects have come via referrals from projects that were finished years prior.

❀ Tell Them, and They Will Come

By now we hope you're feeling like no matter what your budget, you can start to do some advertising to spread the word about your new venture. Remember, it doesn't have to be a national campaign to rival that catchy new soft drink jingle; you just need to make sure the folks that matter know that you're around. We've never really seen the "build it and they will come" adage work in the business world if it isn't accompanied by just a little bit of fanfare to make sure the kids know where to find you.

And don't worry if you're starting to think that budgeting for an ad in your glossy magazine of choice is still a few months (if not a year) away. My dears, that's what public relations is for! And wouldn't you know it? That's the next chapter. Funny how that works, isn't it?

CHAPTER 8

Public Relations

WHETHER OR NOT YOU HAVE the budget for a modest—or a pretty darned kick-ass—ad campaign, you're still going to want to keep an eye on handling even the most basic of public relations for your new business. Public relations includes everything from tracking down the journalists and media that matter to your audience, and trying to get them to plug your business when appropriate, to holding major events to make sure you stay present in your customers' minds. Even a casual approach to public relations deserves a place of honor in your overall marketing plan.

It may help to think of PR simply as marketing for a specialized audience; rather than marketing directly to your customers, you're pitching yourself to an intermediary—the press. They're interested in many of the same things your customers are, and will ask many of the same questions. The two biggies are, of course, "What makes your product (or service) unique?" and "Why should I care?" Just like potential customers, they have a short attention span; you only have a brief chance to make a lasting impression. But don't be scared off by that—remember what a PR agent friend of ours once told us: No one knows more about your company than you do, so you're the person best qualified to tell your story.

While we do have some information in this chapter about hiring a pro PR person, should that be the route you take, the advice that follows is mostly geared at DIY strategies that won't cost you a mint.

❀ *Can I Get That in Writing?*

People are social animals. Generally, you can rely on your customers to spread the positive vibe about you and your business, but why not speed up that process? For starters, get yourself some positive feedback straight from the horse's mouth: customer testimonials. Regardless of what kind of business you're running, testimonials are a great thing to save up for rainy days. Not only can you use them in your own promotional materials—ads, media kits, website, brochure, proposals, or heck, even on your store walls—but you can also use them as a kind of personal affirmation on those slow days when things aren't going so hot. (That last one may sound painfully cheesy, but really, some days a girl needs a little *fromage.*)

If you are generally a shy, private, or humble person, gathering testimonials can be a bit nerve-racking at first. You don't want to bother people, right? Wrong. As a general rule, people actually love to talk—give them a venue and soon they'll be telling you all about how your gluten-free petit fours were all the rage at their cousin's baby shower last month. And once you get the hang of it, it will get easier. We promise.

Depending on your situation, there are different ways to solicit the good word. If you run a store, or have a corner of the world that people come into on a regular basis, you can just leave out a kind of guest book that people can sign their own accolades to. Ditto if your "store" is online. There's nothing easier than setting up a form on your site that encourages people to give you feedback. If you're more of a behind-the-scenes, service-oriented person, ask people if they feel comfortable giving you a testimonial once you finish a project or contract with them. Often people will actually gush about how much they enjoy your products or working with you without any prompting; in those cases, just ask if they mind writing it down—or even suggest that you'll write it down for them if they're comfortable with that.

Once you've got them, use your testimonials strategically. Don't just list everything anyone has ever said about you on one long page on your website; highlight the really relevant stuff, or the descriptions that you feel really speak to how you'd like the world to see you, and focus on those. Of course, testimonials from anyone with a name or position that will hold sway with your target market are golden and should be given special attention. So, if you've heard that someone with a degree of fame who has influence over your customers was thrilled with your prowess, make sure you get a testimonial out of it. It's amazing what spreading the word that Pink just picked up a couple of the custom-painted trucker hats you had on consignment in a local store will do for the sale of mesh headwear in town that month.

Another way to get testimonials is to give something to your clients in return. We've seen some great examples of businesses soliciting creative testimonials from customers through contests and the like. They go something like this: "Send in your story of the best thing that has happened to you while wearing a LuckyDevil Charm Bracelet, and win a gift certificate for $75!" or "Write a paragraph about the most memorable dining experience you had at Chez Bridgette, and get a free dinner for two on your birthday." Think of a scenario and incentive that would be applicable to your own business and spread the word. Not only is it a great way to get customer feedback and testimonials, but you can bet that if the prize is coveted enough, your customers will spread the word about the contest and therefore your business to their friends.

IT'S ALL ABOUT THE LOVE

So getting reams of happy-go-lucky, sweet, and adoring fan-mail-type testimonials is a pretty enticing thought, but what if people have something bad to say about you? Depending on the volume of business you're doing, chances are there are going to be some complainers in the bunch, and opening up the doors for feedback will bring them front and center. And let's face it: No one likes to read criticisms of their efforts. But don't get too hung up on it. Try to keep your perspective when reading both positive and negative feedback and see what of each is worth listening to. Most importantly, don't let your fear of a few bad apples stop you from getting the goods.

NEW KID ON THE BLOCK

How do you get testimonials if you've just started your business or are printing up brochures and don't even have paying customers yet? Hunt down those folks that you gave free swag or services to when you were testing the waters. Get them to compose an ode to your fabulousness and use those. After all, nothing is truly free these days, and they won't mind doing you a favor in return for your generosity. Or if you think your target market can handle a good dose of sass, be really tongue-in-cheek about it. For example: "Aunt Annie just can't get enough of this hemp-based lube!" If done well, it can help to build your brand and will help you stand out from the pack.

❄ *Rewards for Good Behavior!*

The contest framework doesn't really work for our own business—write us a story about the most fun you've had with your website and get a free email form!—but we still take care to reward our clients who spread the love. While new clients come to us through many different channels, there are times when we've had people beeline in our direction precisely because a friend or colleague has told them to. We always ask people how they heard of us, and when it's been through a direct referral like that, as soon as we get the contract we generally send a huge bouquet of flowers directly to the source. After all, if people were inspired to send some business our way once, why not make it a memorable experience for them so they do it again (and again)? It's all about the love, baby.

Those kinds of referral promotions and rewards programs, whether they're formalized or more ad hoc like our own, can also be a valuable tool for promoting your business. Setting up a program where you reward customers for referrals is a great way to use your existing customers to market your business, and retain existing customers by rewarding them for their loyalty. Everything from programs like giving people passes to bring in a friend for a free yoga class to offering a discount to customers if they bring a friend to a sale are easy ways to increase the volume of people through your doors—and money in your pocket. Our chiropractor, who is still in the early years of establishing her practice, sends a gift certificate for a free pedicure to patients who have sent in several referrals. Take a look around at what other people are doing, and then think about what would be most applicable to your business.

▶ Two of the businesses we spoke with—RePlayGround and Rose Flash—use reclaimed and recycled materials as the building blocks of their product lines. As a result, the designers rely on finding intriguing raw materials to work from. Creative women that they are, they've each recruited customers in their quest for materials, offering product credits in exchange for the legwork. It's a win-win arrangement.

❋ *Stop the Presses!*

While advertising, promotions, and word of mouth are all important pieces in your marketing plan, nothing brings on a spike in sales like an article about your business. Effectively one great big testimonial, getting your business written up in a relevant publication, or mentioned as a part of a TV spot, will alert many new customers to your existence and let your current customers know that they're in on a good thing. Here again, networking and connections may be the fastest way to seeing your name in lights. But if you don't already know someone who writes for the local scenester weekly, or have an in with the most relevant trade magazine for your industry, there are other ways to score some coverage.

Depending on where you're trying to get covered, you may be able to be your own PR agent; you might even be able to write the article yourself. Say you want to get some coverage of your fabulous new cookbook: Try contributing an article—or better yet, some recipes—to a targeted magazine or webzine. Perhaps you can even get a column in which you become the resident food expert!

If you don't want to write the article yourself, then you are going to need a press kit. A press kit is kind of like one of those geography reports from elementary school, complete with photocopied bits of magazines and background information on the subject at hand: you and your business. Fortunately there is no diorama component required, but you will want to include product samples if that's your focus, or maybe some kind of catchy, memorable gift that will make the overworked journalist on whose desk your baby will arrive sit up and pay attention. (Tip: If you're targeting high-circulation magazines, you may have trouble competing with the press kits big companies put together for magazine editors. Consider doing a bit of research to get the name of an editorial assistant in the appropriate department— the assistants are less inundated with product samples and swag, and are more likely to pay attention.) Your press kit should include some background information about you, the company, and your products or services, as well as copies of any past press coverage you have had. While the image of the reporter rushing to be the first to get the scoop may still be somewhat relevant at the hard-news desk, the business, style, or food reporters you're likely to be targeting are more into watching trends, and showing them that you're already garnering attention somewhere else will help sell your story. One final tip: Always write "requested sample" on the package you send, even if you're sending it off blind. Magazines get so many samples and packages that a lot of them, sadly, go straight in the bin, unless you make someone take notice.

In addition to the basic backgrounder stuff, be sure that in your press kit you include not only a description of your products or services but the hook behind what makes yours a good story. Another angle to keep in mind is basing your press pitch on an event, be that a fund-raiser, an open house, a conference you're speaking at, or a pancake breakfast featuring the fabulous vegan pancake recipe to be found in your cookbook. While it may increasingly seem like the media is just one big advertisement, they can't help you sell your product if you don't give them a little something to go on. Remember: If nothing else, capitalize on the fact that you're an independent woman running a business; while it shouldn't be news anymore, it sadly still is in many fields, especially if you're going to the mainstream media. So, use that to your advantage.

▶ Megan, whose company The Organized Knitter makes highly coveted needle cases, contributes articles and patterns to magazines like *Craft* and Knitty.com. By establishing herself as a knitting lover within the community, she's helping to build a name for herself and her business.

Do you need a PR person?	
You *may* need a PR person if:	You *don't* need a PR person if:
• your business needs coverage from the mainstream media; for example, the major fashion/lifestyle magazines, national newspapers, or big-time television outlets;	• you can get by with write-ups in the local rags, or independent/smaller-circulation magazines, with maybe a mention or two on the radio or the local cable channel;
• dealing with the media is taking precious time away from your business;	• you send out a press release once in a blue moon;
• you're intimidated, overwhelmed, or just plain turned off by dealing with the media;	• you're comfortable doing your own PR work (or are willing to learn the ropes);
• you're planning a major event at which you'd like some media presence.	• your idea of a major event is an open house where you invite some friends and colleagues around to check out the new office.

❋ *Bringing in the Big Guns?*

Several of the small business owners we spoke to in the course of writing this book summed up the PR question thus: "Until you're ready to be on *Oprah*, you can do your own PR." In fact, many who had worked with PR agents said that if they could do it all over again, they'd hold off on paid PR until later in the life of their business. Their top reasons: It can be expensive, with a long (and tough to quantify) return on investment—but more importantly, your PR agent drives the public image of your company, and if the agent gets it wrong, you'll have a lot of damage control on your hands. Those who've had negative experiences with PR companies will tell you to do it yourself—but it can be a daunting task if you've never talked to the press before.

While you really can get a long way by doing your PR in-house, you may well reach a stage in your business where hiring a professional is the better option. Depending on what league you want to play in—like if you really think you do have a shot at *Oprah*—this may be a necessity. You won't get past the front lobby of some of the bigger media outlets if you don't have a professional on your side who can both craft your media package and use established connections to get you in the door. It generally takes time to see results when working with a PR person or firm; they'll want to work with you to develop a strategic plan.

If you can't (or don't want to) hire a full-time PR person, consider working with one to plan a specific event or to develop a one-time promotion. Another option is to hire one to train you on how to deal with the media. We've done this ourselves, and we learned a ton about how to craft a story so that it has media appeal, as well as how to present ourselves effectively in interview situations.

As with hiring any consultant, you will want to take a look at the person's work beforehand. With a PR company, you are also going to want to consider whether or not their existing clients are your competitors—it will be hard for them to represent you and your competition at the same time. Finally, you'll want to be sure that your business suits the firm; many PR companies specialize in a particular area (such as kids' products, or fashion accessories), and every PR person has a unique style of working. If your PR people don't get you, you'll never see your company's image reflected the way you'd like in your press coverage.

❀ Time for a Nap?

Tired yet, you little social bunny, you? All this glad-handing and cold-calling to "important" people to make sure they're aware of just how fabulous you are starting to take its toll? Well, time for some downtime, sweetie; you deserve it. By this point you're probably starting to see the benefits of hiring professionals to do all this legwork for you, but the hard truth is, in your first few years you may be doing much of this work yourself. Just make sure it isn't going to totally tap you; otherwise you *must* build hiring some pros to help out into your budget.

So rest up, sugarplum! We're not done with you yet. Before we can put this section to bed, we still need to cover the miraculous low-cost marketing tool that probably resides in your very own address book. . . . Networking: It's not just for Amway anymore.

CHAPTER 9

Networking

❀ *Winning Friends and Influencing People*

If you are the kind of gal who absolutely loves getting to know the stranger next to you on the airplane, has an easy time making friends in new crowds of folks, or is a natural public speaker, this chapter will be a walk in the park. You'll just need to focus on making sure that you get your message right to maximize your natural born networking superpowers. For some of you, though, the idea of getting out and mingling for the sake of putting food on your table may make you think twice about leaving your day job. If you're starting to feel queasy already, just remember, like marketing, when you're the boss you can make networking look however you want it to. The key to making it successful will be to find the kind of networking that doesn't make you hyperventilate.

❀ *It's All about Who You Know*

The situation you find yourself in when you first start your business is going to have a big impact on what your existing network looks like. If you're leaving a job where you can take a couple of your clients with you, then you may already have proven customers in your network. Remember: No matter how amicable or acrimonious your situation with your now former boss may be, you need to be above board and professional with both your boss and your clients about your situation. If you are able to take a portfolio of some of your past work with you (even if you can't take the clients themselves), be honest in crediting where it came from—and clear that with your ex-boss.

> *Hannah Howard, of Lizzie Sweet Beauty Products, has the chance to work with stylists all the time at her daytime gig at a record label. Everyone there knows about her side business with Lizzie Sweet, so no one minds when she slips a little free product to the stylists or industry folks she's in contact with. Her advice? "Just make sure you always have some product—or at least business cards—in your pocket! You never know when you'll run into someone who you'll want to have some."*

If you don't already have a few clients up your sleeve, or a good hookup like Hannah Howard, and are really starting from scratch, the next place to look is to your friends, family, neighbors, and acquaintances. Now, you may be thinking we're nuts; what after all would your uncle Mike, who works in a mill and spends his weekends on a Ski-Doo, want with a set of teacups from your Shabby Chic boutique? Well, you might be able to skip Uncle Mikey—though he has to get gifts for his girlfriends sometimes, doesn't he?—but you really never know who other people have in their circles, and friends and family are often happy to brag about their niece or friend in the big city and her business.

All it takes really is a simple conversation: The next time you run into that person who used to trade notes with you in stats class on the street, see a cousin at a family function, or run into your neighbor in the laundry room, let them know what you're up to these days. And if you really think the person is strategic, don't be afraid to ask them to take a little action on your behalf.

Let's say you know your neighbor upstairs is in the film industry (an all-too-likely scenario in Vancouver), and you've just opened a new chic clothing store selling your own line and those of other local designers. Well, make sure you tell the neighbor all about the store, and maybe suggest cheekily that if she can bring down a few of the wardrobe folks you'd happily give them a few items at cost. Or if you've started up a groovy little neighborhood flower shop, don't be afraid to call up your cousin Wes, the investment banker, to remind him where to go when he wants to show his administrative staff how much they're valued.

If you don't see obvious connections, just begin by telling everyone you know that you've started your own venture. You do not have to make them feel beholden to supporting you or rope them into purchasing your product or services if you genuinely think they aren't interested, but keep in mind the fact that each one of your friends and relatives has many acquaintances out there, and if you sell the people close to you on what you are doing, they will spread the word for you.

❁ *Perfect Strangers*

All right: You've sent the family letter home to Spokane, you sent the email around to all your friends, and you're pretty sure you managed to tell everyone in your Pilates class—now what? Check your breath and tuck in your shirt; it's time to make new friends.

As we mentioned earlier, this may be the really scary part for some of you, but you can ease yourself into this stuff. When we first started Raised Eyebrow, aside from the one client we took with us, we needed to start doing something to get some work into our little corner of Lauren's bedroom, and fast. We started by going to networking and meet-and-greet types of events held for our industry. These professional association events were a great way for us to meet like-minded business folks (more on making friends later) and to test the waters and exercise our networking muscles. It was a great way for us to practice our response to "So what do you do?" now that the answer was a bit more complicated than "I work for an IT company"—and allowed us to feel a bit more comfortable with the whole trading business cards thing (though we both still regularly forget to bring them to these kinds of things).

We quickly realized, however, that hanging out with a bunch of other IT professionals wasn't going to be the best way to get clients—many of those gals could build their own websites—so we started to look elsewhere. We accepted invitations to fund-raising events, and Emira started to attend a Business Networking Breakfast group organized by the local Gay and Lesbian Business Association. We had varying success at these kinds of functions. At many of them, we felt strangely out of place at first—often everyone was wearing suits, and our locally designed, deconstructed outfits suddenly didn't seem so chic. And at one wine and cheese event at a local gallery, where everyone was wearing name tags, we must have been asked by a dozen people what range of aesthetics services we offered (people seemed to focus in on the Eyebrow part of our name and ignore the "web studio" that followed it). Once we started to actually play along and discuss waxing techniques with a room full of lawyers, we knew it was time to go.

Often we would leave these events wondering if we were going about things the wrong way; should we be buying "power suits" and ditching our pink business cards for something a little safer? Then we learned our lesson. We were attending a big fund-raiser for a women's charity that was attended by hundreds of professional businesswomen and local celebrity-type folks (think newscasters and columnists). Once again we found ourselves feeling a bit awkward, clutching our glasses of white wine in a crowd of well-tailored skirt-suits; then a woman walked into the center of the crowd wearing a fuchsia mohair jacket, cat's-eye glasses, and fabulously outrageous shoes. We vowed that if we did one thing that afternoon it would be to meet her. We asked our friend, who was one of the gala organizers, to introduce us, and soon found out that she was a marketing professional who regularly hired web designers. She became one of our most beloved and regular clients.

Scoring that client was certainly a bonus for our cash flow, but we learned something way more valuable from her that day: Don't be afraid to stand out. After all, we're web designers, not newscasters, so we don't need to look like we belong behind an anchor desk. And while sadly, neither of us has a pink mohair coat, we can play up our personalities and wear things that will generate a bit of a buzz. If nothing else, wearing your favorite pair of red shoes to an otherwise fairly dull event will often cause a few keen-eyed strangers at the canapé table to comment, giving you an icebreaker. And when you hand your pink and orange cards to the mayor's assistant at a fund-raising dinner, he will likely comment on them, but it will help him to remember you. Of course, use common sense. Don't go breaking out your custom latex corset just to get some attention; there is a time and a place for fetish gear and/or your new micro-mini, and it isn't the local Save the Wetlands Ball. And if you're not comfortable standing out in a crowd, this is by all means not the only way to succeed in networking—it has simply been a comfortable way for us to capitalize on our strengths. Yours will probably be different.

We're fortunate in so many ways to have each other for these sorts of things. No matter how confident you are in a crowd of strangers, it can be a bit daunting to attend these things on your own. So if you can, and if it is appropriate, bring along a friend. Often these types of events are actually not the best place for our partners, who may already be a bit burned out on listening to our constant talk about work—so see if you can't rope a friend into being your plus-one. If you're a bit on the shy side and know someone more outgoing, see if he or she would be interested in being your date. Having a friend whom you trust on your arm can do wonders for your resolve.

As you get more clients and customers you will find yourself invited to more and more events of this nature, be they company Christmas parties or open houses. Or you may want to start throwing them yourself. Attending these events can be a very important way to build and maintain your customer base—and, depending on your business, may in fact be where you spend the time and energy others spend on advertising. You might actually even find yourself getting a bit burned out with a few too many dates in your social calendar, especially after you've already put in an eight- (or twelve-) hour day at the office/studio/shop. So feel free to be strategic about which events you attend; don't feel you have to stay all night, and for goodness' sake don't take too much advantage of the open bar—remember, these are people who you need to respect you in the morning.

As you get established you'll become much clearer about where you'll find your ideal customers. If you make sassy punk T-shirts, then going to gigs and hanging out at the local watering hole may in fact be your version of a gala wine and cheese fund-raiser. Or, if you're the queen of handmade pasties—with or without tassels—then you may actually be able to justify an annual trip to Burning Man to show off your wares and make some contacts. Remember, you're reading this book because the traditional methods don't really work for you, so don't just fall back on them; be creative.

🌸 *Two Peas in a Pod*

When you are running a small business, networking is extremely valuable for two big reasons. As we've already covered, it can help to bring you business. Additionally—and this is the part that traditional business books will never mention—working for yourself can be very lonely sometimes. In order to keep up the creative energy and inspiration that you started with, it will be important for you to continue to be inspired. Networking with other folks in similar situations, or just having the chance to get out there and see people, will help to keep you engaged and excited.

As we mentioned above, an easy start to networking can be found in existing professional networking groups. Look up relevant groups in your town and make a promise to yourself to attend an event on a regular basis.

If that approach doesn't work for you—or even if it does—try to envision other creative ways of networking. You have decided to start a business that is a little off the beaten track, so it is possible that traditional networking groups may not serve you. Creative ways of networking can be as simple as volunteering your time with a group that ties in to what you do. Or, if you're really ambitious—or living in a town that doesn't have anything beyond a Rotary Club—start up your own networking group for businesses that do fit your model more closely. Whether it is a wine and cheese night for everyone on your shop's block, an association for other folks in your industry, or one for women in business, you can probably find a common interest to gather people around.

The women we interviewed for this book brought us tons of examples of DIY networks they either started or plugged in to in their communities. Of course there is the now famous Craft Mafia, founded in Austin, Texas, by nine independent businesswomen working in the crafty/creative field. The Craft Mafia, which has since spawned similar groups across the United States, Canada, and the U.K., was begun as a way to pool resources and share information. Grace Bonney of Design Sponge, a woman with a seemingly endless energy reserve, started Business Lady Meet-up nights in New York after attending smaller informal get-togethers with other self-employed gals in her life. Her first night she had seventy women come out, and it has grown like crazy since then. In fact, the New York nights were so popular that Grace is now helping other women start up similar nights across the United States.

> Grace says of the Meet-ups, "Our first Business Lady event was such a positive experience. Everyone was really so excited to be there, and while this may sound like total cheese, there really is a super-powerful force that is created when a bunch of women get together with the shared goal of supporting one another."

If getting a bunch of women together seems like too much work or just doesn't float your boat, you could follow the lead of our pal Alex Beauchamp; she started a virtual networking group for creative gals with her site Another Girl at Play. Another Girl at Play started out fairly humbly as a way for Alex to profile some of the ladies working in creative fields whom she really admired. She quickly found that she wasn't the only one interested in seeing creative women's achievements shared, and the site took off. Now it has grown into an email discussion list as well, where thousands of women struggling with a lot of the same business challenges can share resources and experiences no matter where they are in the world.

While gender clichés are tired, it is true that in many cases, building networks and relying on each other is something that women tend to do really well. Exploit that trait to your advantage.

❄ *Just Get Out of the House, Would You?*

Several years into starting Raised Eyebrow, and after hundreds of hours spent in a room with only each other to marvel at our scintillating wit and charm, we found that we were starting to yearn for those days when everyone in the office would head out after work to blow off steam, celebrate a project, or gripe about the quotidian nature of working life. At the same time, we also realized just how many truly rockin' women we knew working in similar freelancey-type jobs around town, so we spread the word and started up a semiregular women's cocktail hour at a local bar. At first we thought there could be all kinds of business advantages to getting all these incredibly bright women in a room together (and a few solid contracts and projects did come out of those nights), but mostly it turned out we all just really craved being around some like-minded womenfolk to share a drink and work-related stories with. (Or, you know, stories about how some of us really needed to stop dating go-nowhere musicians who relied on our chutzpah to bankroll their beer budgets, but that wasn't so much in the plan.)

We wouldn't trade the freedom of having our own small business for the politics of working in a larger firm these days, but it is really nice to not feel so isolated. And as a small business gal you may find yourself feeling sometimes like you're reinventing the wheel. Keeping in touch with your peers can be a great way to share advice (like swapping phone numbers for a good accountant or lawyer) and keep motivated.

If we haven't already sold you on the value of networking, here's our final pitch: It's cheaper than paying for ad space. When we talk to other small business owners about how they market their business, they almost invariably start out by talking about "word of mouth," which usually involves some form of networking. Whether it was joining a local group (or starting one), or simply sending an email to another business woman they admired from afar seeking advice, all the business gals we know regularly comment on the value of the business connections they've made. If you're at a loss for a place to start, check out the Resource Guide at the end of this book. Remember, you're not in this alone; there are legions of other smart business ladies out there, and in our experience they're all too happy to share and share alike.

❋ *Your Very Own Marketing Plan*

Now we're about to switch gears and move out of marketing territory and into some of the challenges that growing and maintaining a business can bring. Before you dive into the next section, you may want to review the last few chapters and make note of the marketing techniques that fit your business best. Now that you have an understanding of the various options available, it's the perfect time to refresh your memory about those goals and measures of success you put together way back in Chapter 1, and develop a marketing plan that's going to help you succeed on your terms. (So if one of your visions is to have your sparkly vinyl tool belts featured in *Bust Magazine,* you'll definitely want to have a killer press kit in order.) You don't need to do everything at once; set a few priorities and take small, achievable steps. (The O *Magazine* pitch can maybe wait till after you've made the local daily.)

Once you've determined where to focus your marketing energy, don't shy away from bringing your whole self to the task, even if it means breaking the rules of conventional marketing. Always remember that authenticity is the key to really connecting with your customers, so never be afraid to speak in your unique voice. Originality counts, and this is no time to hide your light under a bushel. Your best customers are always going to be the ones who "get" you, so the better you can communicate your passion for what you do, and the vision that fuels you, the stronger your connection will be with the people buying your wares.

Got it? Good. 'Cause now it's time to talk about keeping your business healthy and thriving well into the future.

GROWING AND MAINTAINING

GROWING AND MAINTAINING
Introduction

As we've already said, the push to first write this book came from our hunt for resources to answer questions about *starting* a business in our early days as entrepreneurs. But as the years wore on, we began to notice that we also needed someone to help us answer the questions we had about *maintaining* our now established business. Information about hiring staff (when we started out we actually thought we would never bring on employees), what to do when you have too much business, how to cope with the slow times, and what to do when your budgets no longer line up with reality all became very relevant issues after we got things off the ground. Growth will look different for all of you: from adding new product lines, to increasing the number of stores that carry your wares, to raising your rates and aiming for a higher-paying client. Regardless of how your business grows, the process will certainly bring with it new challenges, questions, and opportunities.

Growing our business was, frankly, a pretty sticky topic for us for the first two years of business. Looking back on those days, it's kind of comical to see our vehement selves insisting that "no, we were just fine the way we were, thank you very much." Little did we know we wouldn't really be given the option of maintaining the small, two-person studio we first envisioned. Eventually, we were just plain too busy to handle the work that was coming in, and we had to hire someone to come in and help. Then that happened again, and soon we needed bigger office space to house everyone. And, while we still don't aspire to become the biggest design studio in town, we eventually had to admit that our resistance to any kind of growth wasn't helping anyone.

Before we head off into advice land, we'd like to take a moment to address the whole concept of business advice—somewhat ironic in a business book, no? Now, as we've said over and over again, we would be nowhere without the advice and support of our friends and colleagues in the business world. That said, from the moment you even mention to people that you're thinking of starting a business, right through your ongoing life as an entrepreneur, people will give you advice. Often. Some of it may be invaluable wisdom that will feel like a much-needed breath of fresh air. Some of it may come from the most unexpected places—chances are your grandma has more practical advice up her sleeve than the typical MBA—and some of it will come from folks who have the business chops to seem impressive but who don't understand your business. And ultimately, that's the key when wading through any advice. Take it with that proverbial grain of salt, and just because some dude made six figures last year in real estate doesn't mean he knows how you should be marketing your doula services. If someone doesn't actually know anything about your business, but they won't stop telling you what to do, thank them, and move along. And, if they always introduce their advice with the phrase "You know what you gotta do . . . " just smile and nod. *No one* knows what you ought to be doing but you.

With that caveat, we've gathered wisdom from some very smart businesswomen who have been through the kinds of growth you are bound to experience, and we hope that their collective experience can help you navigate the challenges that maintaining and growing your business will bring. Oh yeah, and before we're done, we're going to get you to celebrate all that success, because hey—growing your business? How awesome is that?

CHAPTER 10

You Are Your Best Employee

WE'D LIKE TO TAKE THE TIME to introduce you to someone. Her name is . . . well, let's call her Mary Theresa Martyr (that's Mary T. Martyr for short). She's been running her own successful graphic design consultancy for about two years now, and while her first year was a bit slim, now she finds herself with a full roster of clients and never quite enough hours in the day. But that's okay; she works for herself. She adores her business, and it means the world to her, so what's so bad about giving up a few weekends a month to meet some deadlines? And since the Lebanese place across the street expanded their menu, she hardly ever has to have the same thing for dinner twice in one week! Sure, she misses hanging out with her boyfriend, but he's just so cute when he's sleeping that it almost makes up for never going out to shows together—like they used to when she worked for someone else. And that's the thing that keeps her going when she feels like she can't possibly churn out one more creative project for a client and starts daydreaming about maybe making it back to her yoga class for just one session a week: She doesn't work for anyone else anymore. She's her own boss, and all those sacrifices she's making—missing her niece's second birthday, making fast trips to the park with her dog instead of the long walks in the woods they used to take, never being able to shake that winter cold once it sets in—are worth it, because now she's making these sacrifices for herself.

Right?

No, Mary. Wrong.

This chapter is the one, out of this entire wisdom-filled tome, that we want to see most dog-eared and loved on your bookshelf. Bring on the coffee stains and Post-it notes; make this chapter your guiding star, ladies. For if there is one big, flashing pitfall in the careers of the entrepreneurial gals we've known, it has been the ease with which we find ourselves sacrificing our own basic needs in the quest to succeed. And while it may sound as corny as heck, it's true: You are your best employee. Without you, this business would not have started, and if you don't keep putting your vital, fresh energy into it, it will come to a grinding halt. And so, we can't stress enough how important it is to treat yourself like you would an indispensable staff person.

❀ Do As We Say, Not As We Do

The lessons in this chapter may be the most challenging ones you will encounter as a businessperson, and it is entirely likely that you will find yourself having to relearn them a few times along the way; we certainly have. For while you likely have a strong drive to get all the pieces of your business together, and to take care of the administrative details while also serving your new customers and clients, the tasks that always seem to slip down to the bottom of the list are the ones that read, "Take a day off" or "Leave work by 5:00 PM."

Feeling like you need to be attached to your business 24/7 is one of the biggest blind spots of the successful entrepreneur. While we're not encouraging negligence, if you aren't taking time off to rest and recharge, you are putting your business in jeopardy. In a worst-case scenario, that route can lead to a total meltdown, taking you and your carefully built business with it. On a more immediate level, it's going to result in you losing the spark that helped you start all this, finding work a chore, and losing the time you need to pursue extracurricular priorities.

Now, there are plenty of books out there on "work/life balance"— it's a tricky subject to tackle, and we're certainly not saying we've got all the answers to that here—but we can share with you some helpful tips to make sure you are valuing yourself as you build and grow your business.

❁ *Juggling for Dollars*

Back in Chapter 3, when we had you put together financial scenarios, we encouraged you to account for some basic perks like health insurance and holiday time. The tricky part is putting all that into action. It can be hard enough to decide to stick some money into a health plan when you aren't yet making the kind of salary you really want to— and in fact you may want to wait a few months until it does fit into your budget—but if you don't work in some of those benefits early on, you'll never get used to budgeting for them. And if it seems hard to increase your expenses a little to account for perks and benefits, taking holiday time can seem downright impossible, particularly if you're your business's sole employee.

Believe it or not, going back to those financial projections and budgets can often be a good tool for helping you to take some time or money to reward yourself. While it may just seem like columns of abstract numbers, your budget can be an excellent and impartial evaluation tool to help you gauge where you are in the bigger picture. In the best-case scenario, you're on or ahead of your targets, in which case you shouldn't feel squeamish about giving yourself some well-earned rewards. And if you're not on target, then maybe you need to check in on your original plan. If you had budgeted for a fancy new computer this year but are halfway through the year and your old one is still holding up—while it's getting increasingly difficult to start *yourself* up every morning—then ditch the hardware from this year's budget and see if an extra-long weekend and a road trip to visit a friend aren't doable instead.

> ## PAYCHECKS: THE MUST-HAVE ACCESSORY FOR THIS SEASON
>
> *Too many women (and men) we know who run their own businesses see their salary as a negotiable expense at the end of the month. As we brought up in Chapter 3, making sure your own salary is accounted for is vital to building a business that will last the long haul. Now, that doesn't mean that just by writing a salary into your budget, your paycheck will miraculously write itself every month. There may be months that you need to take a slight pay cut to get through, or you may need to reevaluate your salary for a while until your revenues increase, but if you go too many months without getting paid, you're going to find yourself feeling like one cranky employee. And while you can live on credit cards for a while, the interest payments will soon bury you. So even if it means getting a business line of credit to smooth out your cash flow cycles, be sure to make payday a regular occurrence.*

❋ Time To Get Away?

Taking some holiday time may be easy for some of you, but for most entrepreneurs it can seem near impossible. How will the business survive without you? How can you even think of having days with no sales or billable work? What will your customers do without you?

The details here will be quite different for those of you who make a product and sell it wholesale, compared to those running a storefront, or selling a service. But ultimately, the key to taking holiday time—for all of you—will be planning.

Whether that means roping your best friend into minding the shop for a few days, or letting your clients know that for the last week of August you'll only be checking email periodically for "real emergencies," you're going to have to come up with a plan to take some time away to rejuvenate. If you have a business partner this will be a bit easier; you can try taking time off by taking your holidays in shifts. If not, you may need to get creative and ask yourself some questions to figure out when is the best time for you to be absent:

- When are your slow times? For a consultancy like ours, clients are always away at Christmastime anyway, so that's an easy time to shut down the shop for a couple of weeks. For a hairdresser, on the other hand, the Christmas and New Year party season is one of the busiest times of year, so once that rush is over in January, it can be a bit easier to take some time off (especially given the cash infusion that's just come in). If you make a product, the best vacation time may be after you finish a big production run; or better yet, you may want to time your holidays to fall right before you start a new production run or design period, so that you come to it fresh and inspired.

- Are there long weekends you can piggyback on? It may be a few years before you can really take a week or two off all at once—you may in fact need to wait until you've got staff to take that much time off—but don't write off holidays completely. Tack an extra day or two on to a long weekend when people won't expect you to be around anyway.

- Find some backup. Maybe this means getting your sister to watch the store while you're gone or hiring some temporary help, or maybe it means letting your clients know that in a pinch your friend who runs a similar business across town can help them out.

- Ask yourself what would really happen if you weren't there to answer the phone/emails/etc. for one week. Will it be such a disaster, really? Remember, even neurosurgeons take a few days off to golf. Chances are, if you really check in with yourself on this, the answer is that things will be just fine.

- Set up a regular time off so your customers expect it. Whether it's that you're always closed for the month of August, or that you close at 2:00 on Mondays and Tuesdays, if you're building a regular clientele they will appreciate having regular times when you are and aren't available.

WORK = MONEY

We all know time is money, and for those of us with service- or consulting-based businesses, or for those of you who need to shut down the shop when you're away, taking time off means fewer hours in the month to bring in the rent money. After all, we can't just beg our little sister to build a website or two over the week while we get some R & R. So how do you manage the lost income of vacation days? Well, for starters, when you were planning out your income and expenses waaaay back in Chapter 3, you should have been factoring in a few vacation days/weeks, remember? When you're the boss you'll be the one in charge of making sure there's a bit of cash stashed away in savings to cover things like slow times and vacations. Or, if that's not realistic, but you absolutely need to go to your best friend's wedding in Utah this summer, then you may have to use your line of credit or credit cards to finance a bit of downtime.

While all the hard work of starting up a business, and the perhaps harder work of keeping it going for the first few years, may find you dreaming of sandy beaches, cocktails, and some time alone with a stack of really good books and trashy magazines, that kind of luxury may be a few years off. And sadly it's not just the tropical setting part that will be a challenge. Taking any extended time off just may not be a possibility for you for a while, but don't let that deter you from taking some breathing room. Even if it just means taking one Friday off a month to sleep in and do a self-guided gallery tour or day hike, be sure to take the time off before you end up having a meltdown and need a week under the covers to recuperate.

BUT IT ALL FALLS APART WHEN I LEAVE!

Okay, so that may be true. Whether it's that the messages on your voice mail overload the system if you shut the salon down for more than two days, or that the store's sales take a serious nosedive every time you take a week off to go on a buying trip (let alone a holiday), you need to find solutions to make sure that things don't fall apart when you aren't around for a while. Whether that's checking the messages from the road, or making sure you have the kind of staff you can trust while you're away (what are you paying these people for, after all?), you need to find solutions to make time away from the business possible.

❋ Whatever Happened to Recess, Anyway?

Remember recess? That time when you got to run around, swing from the monkey bars, and have a few cookies with your pals? And whatever happened to the elation of skipping class and playing hooky? Well, in the traditional business world there doesn't seem to be too much of that (and for some cruel reason they also seem to have done away with nap time), but now that you're the boss, you may want to check in with your nine-year-old self and see what she has to say about sitting at a computer all day.

While extended holidays are swell and all, what about the days, weeks, and months in between? Often one of the big attractions to being self-employed is setting your own hours, but the cold reality of running your own show is that that often doesn't seem to translate into any kind of flexible playtime. But it can. There are all kinds of stats to show that even the most overachieving of us can't actually be 100 percent effective forty hours a week, fifty-two weeks a year. Maybe it's time to bring recess back into the mix.

Think about what kinds of little things you really love that would recharge your batteries in those low times. For example:

- We know an extremely successful marketing queen who rewards herself for the very long hours she pulls most every other night of the week by clocking out at noon on Fridays and taking in a matinee solo. While she can't change the long hours every other day of the week, she has managed to get her clients used to the idea that she's never around on Friday afternoons (though few of them know where she goes!).

- Grace, from Design Sponge, describes herself as taking daily minivacations in addition to a week off here and there. She tends to be up and at 'em early and knows she has a habit of staying at the computer way past 5:00 PM, so instead of burning herself out, she regularly takes a few hours off during the day. "It feels so luxurious to be off while everyone else is at work!" she told us.

- Teri Dimalanta of Giddy Giddy splits her workdays up so she can spend the days at home with her young girls. She starts her workday early before they're up, and then picks it back up again in the evenings when her husband gets home. That kind of nonstop schedule may not sound like much of a holiday, but it does allow Teri to build her business while still enjoying hands-on time with her daughters.

Being the boss of you often forces you to be creative, and finding ways to take time off while still keeping the business afloat is just one example. If none of these options work for you, come up with your own: Work four ten-hour days and take the fifth off, or open the shop late on Monday mornings so you can take an invigorating yoga class, and stay later on Fridays to make up for it. Even working small things into your schedule that afford you some downtime will pay off in the self-care they provide. If you're sitting there fretting about all that work that still needs to be done, take a deep breath: If there's one thing that holds true for all the business gals we know, it's that in the end, they *always* get the work done.

❀ *Time after Time*

As we already mentioned, not everyone can be productive 100 percent of the time; we all know that. That said, we can't necessarily just close the doors whenever we feel we're not really giving it our all, can we? So if you find that day after day, when it comes to quitting time, you've been very "busy" but you haven't managed to get anything done, it may be time to take a look at whether or not you're taking the right approach.

In our third and fourth year of business we found ourselves really busy and really, really burned out. Self-care is one of the biggest hurdles we've faced in being our own bosses, and it took us close to two years, and a few very ugly breakdowns, before we got things back on track. The most frustrating part of that time period was not just how much we were working, but how little good work we were actually getting done. That's not to say that we were doing bad work all the time; it's just that for the sixty hours a week we were actually in front of the computer, we were not getting in a good sixty hours of productive time. For every extra hour we worked, we probably only got twenty to thirty minutes of productive time in—the rest of the time was spent grumbling over how exhausted we were, or staring at the computer screen desperately trying to access some last vestige of creative juice. Problem is, the longer you stay at work, the harder it becomes to know when to leave.

However, when you are working on a deadline (or five), and it is your business and reputation on the line, it's hard to clock out at five when the work isn't quite done. Thing is? You probably should. Now, there will certainly be the occasional time that you pull long hours, and sometimes a few late nights and weekends are warranted, but they simply cannot become the norm. After all, if you had a staff person and you regularly required her to work fifty or sixty hours a week, you would probably either want to give her a very serious pay raise, or take a more practical route and hire some part-time help to share the load.

If you find you've got too much to do and not enough time to do it, there are a few things you should evaluate to see if you can't make better use of the hours you do have in a day:

- *Get a virtual secretary.* Not a femmebot, silly—all that technology around you that is so often advertised as being there to make your life easy. If you need a solid four hours a day of uninterrupted time to get your work done, but find yourself distracted by the phone, email, or customers walking in, then try to adjust how you respond to all those little requests. Let the voice mail pick up the phone all day, and only check in on messages/email first thing, at noon, and at the end of the day. You'll be surprised at what a gift all that uninterrupted time is. If letting go of the cell phone that much gives you the heebie-jeebies, then at least start screening your calls for the really important ones. Call display: It's not just for dodging telemarketers anymore.

- *Look after your health.* Dr. Beverley Steinhoff is a brilliant businesswoman and she also just happens to be our cherished chiropractor. (In our line of work, where we work at computers all day every day, a good chiropractor is worth her weight in gold.) When we're pushing ourselves close to the brink, she is often our voice of wisdom, urging us to prioritize physical health and factor it into our business plans. "The best thing you can do for your mental stamina and energy levels is to get into great shape physically—and business owners, who tend to work long hours, especially need to make time for exercise and self-care. You may think you don't have time for it, but you'll gain the time back in increased productivity."

- *Role-play.* Rather than allowing yourself to be pulled in ten different directions all the time—paying bills as they come in, filing receipts, answering the phone, arranging deliveries, and designing your spring line all before noon—try setting up days and times when you'll wear different hats. Plan on using Friday afternoons (when you're usually too burned out to be creative) to take care of bills, invoicing, and going to the bank, and use another morning to take care of all your ordering and other administrative details. Then when these little requests come in during the week, just let people know when you deal with those things; they don't need you to jump to the task immediately.

- *Set expectations.* Let people know that you respond to requests for updates, special orders, or custom work in reasonable time. Depending on what you need to deliver, that may be forty-eight hours or two months. Whatever it is, be sure to give yourself breathing room so that when the inevitable unaccounted-for mishap or interruption arises, you aren't left pulling overtime to meet a commitment you made. Always underpromise and overdeliver: If you happen to get it done early, the customer will be thrilled.

- *Take it where you can get it.* If you find yourself with some extra time one week and know you've got a bunch of heavy work coming up soon, take a day off, knock off early, or take some extra-long lunches.

Jenny Hart of Sublime Stitching, like most of us, has found herself wishing for a few more hours in the day. Specifically, Jenny finds she really needs blocks of uninterrupted time to get certain tasks accomplished. Now that her business has grown, and Jenny has not only the distraction of her email and the telephone but also her coworkers to contend with, she's devised a brilliant system to let others know she needs some private time. She picked up one of those battery-powered lights you tap to turn on—you know, the ones meant to be installed in closets? She has one on her desk that she taps on when she needs to be left alone to get things done, especially when she needs a chunk of creative time. It's like her own personal ON AIR sign that cues everyone in the office that she's not to be disturbed. And, to be fair, she got one for everyone else in the office too.

❀ Please, Ma'am, I'd Like Some More

One of the reasons you went into business for yourself may very well have been to start paying yourself what you're worth. It was certainly a motivating factor for us. And remember the title of this chapter? You are your best employee? Right, well you don't want your best employee jumping ship because the salary and benefits package down the block is sweeter, now do you? (Here's a hint: When you find yourself daydreaming wistfully about the days when you were working for your former boss, it's time to reevaluate your compensation package.)

We had you plan for raises and bonuses in your financial scenarios, and it is important that you implement those—and review them regularly. Whatever your business is, you're also going to have a financial year-end, and that makes for a great time to evaluate how your past year went and to project what you can expect for next year. Imagine yourself going in to meet with your boss, and think about what you would ask for. A raise? An expense account that would allow you to buy books and magazines to keep you inspired? An all-expenses-paid trip to a conference once a year? A better health plan? A company car/bike/bus pass? Check in with your accountant and see what kinds of perks you can write off as legitimate business expenses, and then see what kind of dream package you can give yourself. (If you forget what counts as legit write-offs, flip back to Chapter 3.) It may only start out with a $10-a-week budget for company lunches delivered on Fridays, but start somewhere and let these grow as your business does.

❧ *Power in the Balance*

While we can certainly attest that work/life balance is an absolute necessity for both the short- and long-term health of any business, perhaps the most rewarding part of all this self-care is that you are doing it for yourself. Even the little ways we rewarded ourselves during struggling times in our business—company transit passes and basic health insurance—were powerful. Having the ability and the focus to be the one taking care of yourself can feel incredible, and watching those perks grow over time as your business expands is truly fantastic.

CHAPTER 11
Hiring Help

So you're your best employee: swell. What if you (and your business partner, if you've got one) are simply not enough? After all, no matter how efficient and talented you are, there are only so many hours in a day, and while it is nice to think you can do it all, unless you are some kind of ultra-superwoman you'll probably wind up needing some help here and there (especially when you have to handle all that imminent success!). So at some point—and for some of you, this point will be sooner rather than later—you'll need to hire someone to do something. While this is not a book geared at encouraging massive and rapid growth in the business world—there are already enough books out there doing that—if you're doing things right, growth will happen, and eventually you are going to need a helping hand.

The spectrum of hiring people to help you out is a vast one, and we're going to try to at least touch on all of it here. Whether you are hiring someone for a few hours of their time to help you with your taxes, outsourcing production, or actually taking on full-time staff, there are a number of principles that can help guide you in making good choices when it comes to expanding your business team.

❧ *How to Know if You're Ready*

Bringing in extra help—whatever form that might take—can be very challenging. There's a pleasant certainty in yours being the only personality to manage and account for. And when you're working really hard for the money you bring in, it can also frankly be a bit unsavory to think about splitting some of your hard-earned cash with someone else. The reality of being the boss, however, is that often, by shouldering the entire burden yourself, you might just be doing yourself a disservice.

> *When Jen LaBelle from Romp, a Brooklyn-based toy store, started her business, she knew she couldn't be the only retail gal at the store while she raised her two-year-old. So, in the early days, her mom came on board as her first staff person. (She has since expanded her hiring circle beyond her immediate family.)*

This is one lesson we seem to have to learn over and over again in our own business. For the most part, we always thought we had just about everything figured out. We knew what our specialties were (and what they weren't), and we were pretty good at finding a balance between taking on extra tasks to save cash and hiring experts to take care of things like our year-end taxes that clearly fell outside our skill set. All that considered, however, we still find ourselves from time to time struggling with some things for way too long before we realize that we're not the best people to handle them, as the following two examples illustrate.

▶ *The Number Crunch*

For the first five years of our business, we did all our bookkeeping through some basic spreadsheets, recording expenses and invoices and keeping general track of our cash flow. Then, at the end of the year, we would bundle up all our sorted receipts and Excel files and send them to our fabulous bookkeeper, who would then call us a few weeks later with a tax return ready for us to sign. We didn't need to stay on top of tax law, and we had a fairly simple system for tracking our basic company finances, so we always knew how we were doing.

However, after five years in business, things started to get a bit more complicated books-wise, and we started to think that keeping track of things in a bookkeeping program—like QuickBooks—was a good idea. We consulted with our accountant and she agreed. So Emira, who takes care of our daily finances, set out to buy the software, install it, and get it up and running. She figured an afternoon would do the trick; after all, we're very comfortable with computers, and new software and math have always been among her strong suits. She was wrong. Several days into tearing her hair out trying to figure out a bunch of accounting terms that she only had vague ideas about—trial balance, anyone?—she lost it and broke down. After talking things through with Lauren, she realized that it didn't matter how good she was with numbers and computers; there was a learning curve here that was going to take much more than an afternoon to get over. Twenty minutes later, a call was made to the accountant, who laughed and said that she could get the program all set up and running in an hour and then come in and do an hour or so of training to get us up and running—all for a screaming deal.

▶ The Wisdom of Crowds

For nearly two years we found ourselves working way too many hours, and enjoying our work less and less as we rushed from deadline to deadline; we were always playing catch-up and never felt like we had the chance to get into big-picture questions or have a bit of fun with our work. We asked pretty much every successful businesswoman we admired what she recommended to cure our work life, which had gotten truly out of balance. Time and time again, they all asked us if we had considered hiring staff, and we vehemently said no. We wanted to stay small, and we were worried about upsetting our great working relationship with one another by adding another person into the mix.

Eventually, though, we reached our breaking point and decided to give it a try. After crunching some numbers to make sure we could actually pay someone, we hired someone on a part-time contract to help out twenty hours a week. Almost immediately things began to turn around. We went back to a reasonable workweek, had time to plan and be creative again, and in fact our cash flow also improved, as we were able to complete projects more efficiently and take on more work. Six months into the contract, we brought that person on as a full-time employee. That lesson took us about two years, and the advice of literally dozens of super-smart business folks. We hope to spare you the pain.

❀ What Is Your Time Worth?

Whether you're thinking about using a bookkeeper to do your taxes or taking on an intern to help you sew zippers into your purses, one of the first questions you should ask yourself is, What is my time worth? Sure, you can paint the office yourself, and if cash is tight you just might want to do that, but if it is going to take you two days to do that and you bill out at $75 an hour, then maybe you're better off working from home for a day or two and hiring a professional or friend to do the grunt work for you.

❀ Am I the Best Person to Do This?

Maybe you're not a details person. Or maybe you *are* a details person, but there's a job to be done quickly that really doesn't require a perfectionist's touch. Maybe you've got a task that demands a level of expertise that you a) do not have and b) are not interested in acquiring. While the old adage "If you want something done right, do it yourself" may be true some of the time, we can't all be Jills-of-all-trades. While we certainly fancy ourselves to be talented gals, we realized early on that we were best to hire someone else to do our logo and identity work; not only are we a bit too close to it to be impartial judges but we are not really logo designers by trade and our image was important enough to us to hire a pro. Likewise, Aimee Dolby, whose company Betsy Ross makes stylish and easy-to-sew clothing patterns, didn't let her lack of formal training as a pattern drafter stop her from starting her business. She knew there would be a demand for her designs, so she hooked up with a woman who could do the pattern grading required to realize her vision.

❧ But Mom! Do I Have To?

So one of the big perks of being the boss of you is being the one who gets to say who does what when, right? Right. So if you really hate doing something, we mean *really hate it,* don't do it. Find someone else who can. (Just be sure to build this into your budgeting.) Of course, if you really hate going to press proofs, then you probably don't want to be a graphic designer, so use your common sense here. But don't force yourself to do something just because you think you *should.* You're the boss now; you set the rules.

❧ Taking the Big Leap: Hiring Staff

As we alluded to early in the chapter, hiring staff was a big deal for us. It may not be such a challenge for you, and in fact you may not be able to wait nearly as long as we did. (Typically retailers, or any kind of manufacturing business, will need to bring in help much earlier than a consultancy like ours.) But in the event that taking on staff is a hurdle for you, we'd like to help you sail over it. (Ahoy! Pep talk ahead.)

❈ *The Boss of Them*

When you think about hiring staff, does it just feel like one big scary list of stuff to do? (Figure out a job description, manage their time, teach them how to do the job, check in on their progress, find the money to pay them, and so on.) Often when you're really busy and overworked—which by the way is exactly when you need some staff—it can be really hard to think about adding any other tasks to your week. The thing to remember—this may seem obvious now, but when you're in the thick of it, reality becomes a little blurry—is that the staff person (or people) you bring on will also be taking some of that work off your plate. If the person you hire is not making your days easier, you need to fire him or her and find someone who does.

Beyond all the concrete excuses about how it would take too much time to hire and manage someone, and how our business was really about us—and how would we possibly find someone who was "like us"?—there was some pretty basic authority-issue-type stuff holding us back as we continued to delay the hiring process. By the time we got to the point of running our own business, we had both had our share of "bad boss" experiences, some of them more nefarious than others. And while we could be pretty certain that we would never be the kind of bosses to throw things around the room or buy expensive luxury vehicles while underpaying our employees, the easiest way to avoid being a "bad boss" was really to just never be one. So while we had all the work of figuring out payroll and labor law to consider, we also needed to do some personal growth work to really figure out what kind of bosses we wanted to be, and just how we would make sure we achieved that. We were lucky enough to have a brilliant business coach, who actually breathed a huge sigh of relief and said "Finally!" when we asked her to help us hire staff, and we brought our fears and problems to her. (For more about just what the heck a business coach is, see Chapter 14.) There are also lots of great books and resources out there on what the business world refers to as HR (human resources), which can offer you advice on how to manage people well so that you don't become that loser who drives her employees to drink. (Check out the Resource Guide for HR tips.)

Once we did all the hard calculations to prove that we could indeed afford to take on a part-time staff person—Iordisa, do we love a good spreadsheet!—Emira thought her fears about hiring would vanish. But as the interview days (and the starting day for our chosen candidate) loomed, she realized she still hadn't reconciled all her issues about being someone's boss. She was definitely looking forward to having an extra someone to share the workload, but whenever anyone used that "boss" word, she got a bit queasy. For Emira, this was a really muddy personal struggle composed of ghosts of bad past bosses, fears around not being ultimately responsible for the work that comes out of our studio, a general distrust of authority, and a touch of concern that at twenty-nine years old (her age when we made our first hire) she had no business calling someone else her "employee." Fortunately, Lauren's support combined with our employee's total fabulousness made the real-life transition pretty easy to handle, but it definitely took some serious work on Emira's part to make it doable.

Hiring staff is also a great opportunity to ask your other brilliant business owner friends for their equally brilliant advice. Once we decided to make this leap, we went back to all our colleagues who had been urging us to do so for so long. If you don't know many other business owners, have no fear. Call up that friend of yours who is always raving about how much she loves her job and take her out for lunch. While she may not be able to give you advice on payroll taxes, she will be able to tell you just what it is about her work environment that makes her such a happy camper. Take notes!

❋ *Staff vs. Contractors*

As you are doing your initial hiring, it may be worth considering whether or not you can bring on somebody on contract, or if you need to actually hire that person as an employee. There are many legal considerations here around employee standards, and as a boss it is your very real legal responsibility to look into the particulars in your part of the world, but we'll go over some of the big things to consider as you start to evaluate the choices that face you.

When it is great to bring on a contractor:

- *You need help in the short-term on a project with fixed start and end dates.* Whether that means an extra pair of hands to deal with Christmas orders, or to work on a large consulting project, if you don't have ongoing work for an employee but just need a hand getting through a job, a contractor may be for you.

- *You need someone with a skill set you don't have to complete a task/project.* Consultants will regularly partner with other consultants to complete a project. Sometimes that team is put together by the client; sometimes your client wants you to put that together, in which case you are responsible for hiring the other contractors. If you are manufacturing a product, you may contract out a piece of the production: the fabric screening, the pattern drafting, or putting in those damn zippers.

- *You do not have the space or funds to bring someone in–house.* Contractors can be great, as they often (and, generally, are legally required to) work from their own office space/living room, reducing your financial responsibility to increase your overhead and provide the space and tools required for them to do their job.

When you should look at hiring staff:

- *You have too much work. All the time.* An ideal problem to have in many ways, though stressful all the same. Some of you will know from the get-go that you'll need staff to keep this ship afloat, either in the form of an assistant, someone to watch the shop while you take a day off here and there, or as another piece of your business puzzle. Others of you will gradually come to this place as your business grows. And for some it may literally happen overnight when you get a big contract/picked up by a major retailer/profiled on *Oprah*. Regardless, if it is clear that you've got more work than just you can handle as far as the eye can see, then it is time to bring on staff.

- *You need someone in–house.* Legally, if you are bringing someone in to work in your office/shop/studio on a regular basis, then you need staff. You may be walking some fine lines here, so do look into the legalities of this for your own case, but if you bring someone in on contract who really should be an employee, you can get nailed (i.e., audited) come tax time. Yikes!

THE GOLDEN RULE OF BILLABLE TIME

Okay, so maybe this isn't a classic golden rule, but as far as advice goes it is easily worth its weight in gold. As a service-based business, when you are looking to bring on staff because you can't handle your workload anymore, you are going to need to look at what work you want them to do. After all, there are likely hundreds of tiny little tasks that make up your day, and you could offload many of them onto someone else's to-do list. Our first instinct was that it would be much easier/less risky to offload nonclient work, like administrivia and paperwork, onto an assistant rather than involving her with our clients. We asked some colleagues with a similar business model who had recently hired staff, and they emphatically stopped us in our tracks. "Your staff must do billable work," they told us, "otherwise it is much harder for their work to pay for itself." That is, it's much easier to pay your new employee's paycheck if the work she is doing can directly increase your revenues, whether that's by contributing to client projects, making sales, or helping you get your products out the door. That extra income she's generating can go toward paying her wages, whereas if she's answering your phone or organizing your file cabinet, she's not necessarily helping to boost your bank account balance. For us, the trick to this was that we needed to have enough extra billable work for a staff person to take on while we continued to meet our own targets for billable work, but given the fifty- and sixty-hour weeks we had regularly been pulling, that wasn't too tricky. For product and retail businesses the same kind of rule can apply, just in slightly different ways. Your staff should make it easier, faster, and/or more efficient for you to get your product out the door or to serve more customers, and therefore bring in more money to pay their wages.

❁ *The Pros and Cons of Both*

There are definite benefits to both sides of the hiring coin. Contractors can place less strain on your business, but are less predictable. Staff can be more reliable, but come with their own costs. Here are some comparisons of the relative merits of each:

	Contractor	Staff
Reliability	Contractors aren't all totally unreliable flakes (though we've met our share of those), but by nature of your relationship with them they can be less predictable. They likely don't (and shouldn't) work on-site, so you aren't able to manage their time/attention too closely. Depending on your agreement with them, their level of responsibility for getting the job done on your terms can be limited.	Accounting for sick time, and unexpected emergencies, staff are generally pretty reliable. You can plan what work you need them to take on, and once you get a sense of their work style and competencies you'll be able to predict how much work they can take on. As your employees they are highly accountable to your needs.
Availability	Availability will really vary dramatically from contractor to contractor, but a common problem with relying on excellent contract workers is that they get busy, and not just with the work you give them. Unless you have a really predictable contract with your contractor, and open communication about their other workloads, you might not be able to count on them for short-notice work.	While employees always have the right to quit, you can generally get a pretty solid sense of how much work you can take on and what your ongoing capacity is when you have employees to rely on.

	Contractor	Staff
Overhead Cost	Not having to worry about payroll costs (income tax, Social Security, Medicare, vacation pay, etc.), benefits, and the overhead involved in keeping an employee makes contractors very appealing. No matter how big your business grows, you will likely find that sometimes it makes more financial sense to hire contractors for certain tasks.	There's no doubt about it, employees are expensive. Often they are a necessary and important expense to pay (like rent and the phone bill), but they will increase your operating budget. Wages are often the largest expense of a business.
Predictable Expenses	While contractors can certainly be less of a drain on your overhead costs, they can be hard to predict, budgeting-wise. Just because you had someone do a similar job for one price doesn't mean that someone else (or that same person) may not charge more next time around.	You will need to account for raises, and unexpected expenses always seem to arise in business, but when you have a salaried staff person, you can get a pretty solid sense of your labor costs.
Multitasking	In most cases, you can't hire a contractor to take on multiple tasks. Typically they are assigned one big task or one major piece of the puzzle to complete.	While you need to have a solid job description for any employee, that outline can cover a lot of ground, having them help you with everything from minding the shop to doing some small production work on slow days.

	Contractor	Staff
Varied Skill Sets	While we're all out there searching for that Jill-of-all-trades who can manage client/customer relations, balance the books, and design your fall line, she likely doesn't exist. The beauty of contractors is that you can take that same budget you would use to hire one salaried employee and split it up among a few expert contractors.	You will probably require your staff people to do a fair bit of multitasking (as described above), but you can't expect them to sprout new skills overnight, and as the needs of your business evolve, you may find your staff resources coming up short in meeting some of your needs.

If you're not careful, contractors can cost you money—above and beyond their fees. This is particularly relevant to service-based organizations and consultancies like ours, but can be true for retail/product-based businesses. If contractors deliver their work late, it can end up costing you more of your time in managing them, fee penalties with the client, or in some cases—like if you are trying to get a product ready to sell—an inability to earn any money at all. This is a hard lesson to learn, and one that you will likely need to learn through experience, but you always need to either pad the cost of a contractor's fees by simply increasing them when you quote a client, or increasing the final cost of your product. In worst-case scenarios, you may even need to fire a contractor who is not performing and hire someone else to finish the job—doubling your costs—so try to give yourself some padding in the budget for mistakes to happen.

❀ How to Hire

Again, there will be all kinds of legalities around hiring someone, which vary from state to state, so you need to do your homework and get those details. Likewise, make sure you are legally covered if you are going to work with a contractor. Pay a lawyer to go over your contracts, or do some hardcore library research on this front; it can save you plenty when and if things go wrong. That said, there are some basic principles you should apply any time you are looking to invite someone to your party.

GET REFERRALS

Whether you are hiring an employee or looking for a really solid bookkeeper, start by picking up the phone and using that network of like-minded folks you know. Although putting an ad in the classifieds, on the notice board at the local coffee shop, or on Craigslist is certainly likely to get the resumes pouring in, you will have to do plenty of culling to get down to the ones that are actually relevant to you—whereas putting out the word to colleagues, friends, and family is likely to get you some much more qualified leads. So just as you'd ask your best friend where she gets her eyebrows done before trusting yours to "Eyebrows 'R' Us" out of the phone book, use your network for referrals. You'll save plenty of time, and it often leads to great results. After all, you're going to rely on word of mouth to spread the word about your business, right?

INTERVIEWS

These can be your formal job interview scenario—you sit down on one side of the desk; they sit on the other—or on the other hand, you may just meet up with someone casually to suss them out. If you're looking for an insurance broker, bookkeeper, or graphic designer, this will probably be a fairly informal process. (For more details on hir-

HIRING YOUR FRIENDS

We talk a lot about relying on the goodwill and awesome skill sets of your talented friends in this book, and we'd be total hypocrites on many counts if we told you never to mix business and friends. (We are best friends and business partners, after all.) But (and you knew there would be a "but") do be careful here. Just as you should always exercise caution when sharing an apartment with your best friend of all time, especially if you know she's a total slob, you should be very careful about hiring friends, family, or close associates. When and if you do, make sure you have a really open conversation about expectations from the outset and set up some clear boundaries about how you would end the working relationship without compromising anyone's feelings. You need to hire this person because you think they have the skill set you need, not because you once shared a bedroom or now share a crush on the lead singer of the local semifamous indie garage band.

ing graphic designers, see Chapter 6.) You can go by their office, or meet for a coffee, and talk about their general approach to their work, what kinds of clients they like to have (remember, when you hire a contractor, you are in a sense the client), and generally get a feel for how they will be to work with. If you are hiring an employee, you will want a more formal process that involves reviewing resumes and scheduling interviews (best held on your turf so they can get a sense of the work environment you are offering—after all, they are also checking you out), after you have been through a pile (or piles) of resumes and selected the most likely candidates. You may also want to do follow-up interviews once you have short-listed from a larger pool. Julia Beardwood, who runs Beardwood and Co., LLC, a design agency in New York, takes bringing on staff very seriously; after all, as she reminded us, "You're going to have to spend a lot of time with them, once they're hired." She goes beyond the interview process to find a way to work with her potential new employees on a trial project basis. That way, she has a chance to see what they are like to work with in a "real life" scenario.

In either case, you need to do some homework to prepare the questions you want answered, give the other person a sense of how long the interview will be (i.e., how much of their time you'll need), and think about what kind of qualities you are really looking for. Our advice when devising interview questions—particularly formal ones—is to stick primarily to professional questions and stay away from too much in the way of "lifestyle" questions aimed at getting at someone's personality. Not only is that kind of rude, but asking many personal questions is actually illegal in a job interview scenario. While it is definitely going to be important to get a sense of what kind of person you are inviting into your company, many of those qualities will probably be revealed in how the interviewee deals with your professional questions. And while it's important to bring in someone you will get along

One, two, three, four, we won't take this anymore. Five, six, seven, eight, we don't discriminate. Okay, we are so very sure that if you picked up this book we do not need to tell you this, but just in case you have momentarily misplaced your brain (and your ethics too), we are going to take a second of your time to remind you that discriminating based on the race, gender, sexuality, or age of a candidate is not only grossly lame but very illegal. That doesn't mean you need to hire someone to answer your phones who cannot speak the language in which you conduct business just because they applied for the job, but for heaven's sake don't let your preconceived notions of the best person for the job prejudice you against making the best hiring decision.

with, this is not online dating. You do not need to know what their sign is (though Lauren's affinity for astrology makes her particularly fond of our Leo employee's loyalty), what their favorite book is, or where they spend their vacations. That said, don't feel like you need to ask typical interview questions if you don't think they will get you the answers you are looking for. Feel free to conduct the interview in the same style that you conduct business, and if that is a bit outside the realm of the straitlaced business world, go for it. Just be sure your interviewee is prepared.

If you are hiring based on resumes—or a call for proposals for a contract—tailor each interview a bit to the information the interviewee has given you in the resume/proposal they submitted. Ask them questions about areas that need more clarification, or that

When we were preparing for interviews for our first staff position, Emira was worried that while we had covered all the "technical" aspects of the job, we weren't asking enough about these people who would potentially be sharing office space with us twenty (and later forty) hours a week. We were very used to having just our two personalities in the room, and as best friends to boot, it was hard to imagine fitting someone else in there. That said, neither of us was comfortable with asking cheesy questions about their favorite hobbies or, heaven forbid, what sports teams they were on in high school. Turns out each interviewee gave us a great sense of his or her personality in the thirty minutes or so it took to get through the interview process. From the guy who showed up in full matching motorcycle gear, including matching green leather pants and helmet, to the woman who told us all about how she really hates being at work before noon and is typically an hour or two late every day, we got a really good sense of each person by the time we were showing him or her the door.

you think are particularly applicable to the work you need them to do. Having them describe their last few jobs/projects will also give you a really strong sense of how they approach their work.

Get References

Okay, so the graphic designer down the hall swears that the girl she had in last summer to help her with a big job will be the perfect fit for your company, and that's a great place to start. That said, if you are going to bring this gal in to share your space and take on your client work, you'll need to know a bit more about her. Beyond the interview, you need some references—and not just one from her mom. This can be a combination of professional and personal references, as long as they answer some of the questions that are essential to the skills you need that person to bring to the job. Everything from punctuality and reliability to specialized knowledge needs to be verified before you start to rely on this person. Sure, she says she's installed hardwood floors before, but there's no harm in talking to someone who paid her to do that and making sure she's just as good at it as she says. You will need to gauge the rigor of your reference checking based on the level of responsibility you expect someone to take. But the cost of a bad contractor or employee is too high not to take the time it requires to really check someone's references.

Get It in Writing

Whether it is a contract for short-term work, or a part-/full-time employee, you need a formal contract between you and your new helper. The contract should benefit both of you, so don't be too surprised if they suggest or require changes to it. You need to be certain that your contracts not only cover the basic legal requirements for your area but also cover the specifics of the scope and type of work you need this person to do for you. If you are hiring staff, you will need to cover the benefits you plan to include, as well as guidelines for sick time and vacation time. And whether you are bringing someone on for the short or long term, you will also need to include details on how the contract can be terminated by both parties should things change or go wrong. There are plenty of legal details to be covered in contracts, and it's really in your best interest to have them looked over by a lawyer—or at least really do your homework. There may also be some small business services in your area that can review your contracts or provide guidelines for you to work from. Just please take the time to do this right; it is well worth the cost of the lawyer's fees to have your backside covered if something goes wrong.

❧ *Treat Your Staff Right . . .*

Becoming an employer requires more than just making the mental leaps required to actually be someone else's boss; it also means you're now legally responsible for another person's welfare in all kinds of ways. We're not going to go into all the nitty-gritty of just what those requirements are here, except to say that you need to find out. (Check our Resource Guide in the back for places to start looking.) There are labor codes to uphold around holidays and medical leave, and federal—and sometimes state—taxes to be paid (and possibly worker's compensation as well), and you need to make sure you're adhering to all the legal guidelines required. Your state's small business development center will have someone who can help you figure that all out and direct you to the right forms and steps to take. Their services are free, and they will be the most up-to-date on all the various levels of government bureaucracy that surround being an employer, so take advantage of them.

Beyond those basics, this is also your opportunity to be that totally awesome boss you always dreamed of. Remember her? She would always appreciate you, give you a company expense account, and every second Friday off. . . . While doing all that for your employees may not be viable if you want to keep the business afloat, do try to remember back to those days when someone else was in control of the day-to-day details of your work life. What you are able to do to make your employees happy is going to look different for each of you, and will vary greatly depending on your cash flow and how much responsibility each staff person is taking on, but make sure you budget both the time and money to treat your employees well. Some stats say that the cost of hiring and retraining new staff is as high as 25 percent of the annual wages of that employee. That's one-quarter of a year's pay each time you have to replace a staff person—and it's basically money lost, since it cuts into your productive time as well as your new employee's. Seen in that light, there is sound financial value in paying your employees well and offering them a decent benefits package and/or job perks. But don't worry; you don't necessarily need to compete with the big companies on these fronts. You're still a small business, after all. Chances are, your staff will choose to work with you because they like the idea of working for a smaller company, and they will get some value from the kind of work environment and philosophy you bring to business. Be sure to check in with them regularly—annual employee reviews are a good idea for everyone involved—and see if there is something you could be doing to make their job better, or life a bit easier. You'll be surprised at how some of the time, something that seems like a small request—everything from being able to play their own music to being able to shift their hours to start and finish an hour later—can be a big deal to your staff.

❋ . . . But Don't Let Them Walk All over You

Being a nice, considerate, and above all respectful employer is very important. That said, you don't want to be a doormat. Nor do you necessarily want to be their best friend; you need to keep your relationship with your employees professional. That doesn't mean that you need to be the ice queen and remain a totally emotionless robot who rules from on high. It's just that your role as boss is not to be your employees' friend, counselor, or mom—they likely have other people in their lives who can take on those roles. Your role as boss is to pay them well, treat them with respect, and value their contribution to your company's success. Whether you do that through praise, monetary reward, or lunch when a big sale comes in or a project is completed (or a combination of the above), just be sure you do that within professional boundaries and that you are both comfortable with the situation. Hint: Taking her and her girlfriend out for a great dinner at the local Italian pasta joint and footing the bill (including a nice bottle of wine) is good; taking just her out to that cozy little Italian bistro, getting messy drunk, and telling her how wonderful and beautiful and fabulous you think she is before dancing on top of the bar at the end of the night is bad.

The best skill you can have in being a good employer is good communication. If you want your employees to take on some tasks that you've previously taken care of, and that fall outside of what they've done in the past, ask them how they feel about it. If they genuinely don't want to do it, and they already have a full workload, then fine. But if you are struggling to get things done and they keep refusing to take things on for you, then you probably need to fire them—or at least have a serious talk about their future. On a smaller scale, you can discuss what things they would like to help out with. While it isn't fair, or particularly good for employee satisfaction, to keep giving your staff tasks that you find too unappealing to do yourself, ultimately they are your staff and they don't get to have total control over their work.

❁ *Who's the Boss Now?*

Working with other people—be they staff or contract workers—can be a really big step in owning your own business and growing into your role as the boss. Whether you need to do this first thing in order to get your business off the ground, or later as your business grows, you need to make sure that you are being the absolute best boss you can be in how you treat both your contractors and staff. That said, do allow for the possibility of making some mistakes—who, you?—as you get used to being someone's boss. Just make sure you do your homework, so they aren't big mistakes that will ultimately cost you. But don't be afraid to apologize if you screw something up, or something doesn't go quite as you planned for your employees; they will appreciate your honesty and reward you with loyalty.

Taking on staff can be about just maintaining a healthy business, affording you time to take off, and making sure you can handle your existing workload. Hiring can also be about growing your business, but it is only one piece of that leap of faith. We've addressed the others in the chapters ahead—things like getting more space and expanding your capacity—so if you think that sounds like it is in your future, stay tuned!

CHAPTER 12

Customer Service

IN ADDITION TO YOUR PRODUCT, your employees (if you've got them), and certainly yourself, one of the big recurring themes in business will be your customers. (Of course, if it isn't, then you may need to go back to the marketing chapters and try to figure out how to get yourself some. . . .)

Whether you call them customers or clients (or something else entirely), these are the people who compose one of the vital pieces of the puzzle when it comes to writing your paycheck each month. Given that these folks are going to become regular fixtures in your life—whether it's for five minutes while they buy their fair trade coffee and spelt breakfast muffin from you or for five months while you work on a major contract—it is worth spending some serious time thinking about how you want those relationships to function.

Good relationships with your customers will help to keep you going as you get out of bed each morning and head into the office/living room to start your day. Growing and maintaining a healthy customer base is going to be one of the key factors in keeping your business strong and healthy over time. If we haven't already said it enough: Good word of mouth is really the best and the cheapest form of advertising there is.

❈ Bring on the Love

After eight-plus years in a consultancy business, and with a client list that is growing well into the hundreds at this point, some days it feels like the "bad clients" are the ones who linger most in the mind— and over Friday-night cocktails with our girlfriends, the stories some- times never seem to end about the ridiculous requests we have fielded (and in some cases, attempted to fill). But, as Monday morning rolls around—and be warned of serious cheese alert here—we both still find ourselves looking forward to the work we have ahead of us. We could be deluding ourselves here, or it may just be pure dumb luck, but we think it also has something to do with having worked really hard at building and maintaining a client base we truly adore.

We didn't really have an explicit plan for how we would do it when we started our business—aside from the fact that one of our big motivators in striking out on our own was to work with clients we loved—but over the years, we have been able to see just how to build and maintain a client list that we love working with. And while we don't have a Cupid's quiver of love arrows to pass on that will magi- cally bring you a similarly delightful group of fabulous customers, we can pass on some tips for growing yourself a group of customers who will actually help you love the work you do.

❈ Why Should I Care?

Now, we're not suggesting that you build yourself a client base of people for whom you just pine and ache, day in and day out, because they are so darn amazing you can't imagine your life without them— or that you start pasting photos of them all over your bedroom wall in a high-school-flashback kind of a way. What we are talking about is finding clients and customers who help you feel good about the work you do, *and* help you make a decent living while you are doing it.

Not all of you are going to have tons of contact with your customers—or maybe you'll only have that contact for three and a half minutes while they grab their wheatgrass shot and run. And, as everyone who has waitressed knows, you can't always control who sits in your section, but chances are your customers are going to play a recurring role in your new life as a business owner. Many of you who have chosen this book are going to be starting a business that in some way expresses something that brings you great pleasure. Whether that's finding a way to make a living from your love of photography or from your affection for writing the best possible press release for your clients, you are probably feeling motivated at this point in your life to make a career out of doing something you love. And we're all about supporting that love.

If you don't find like-minded people who will pay you what you and your products are worth, then your love of that craft is going to take a very quick nosedive. On the other hand, when you do find those customers you adore, it is usually because they understand what you have set out to do—whether that is to sell the city's most delicious and nutritious take-home organic soups or to do the most cutting-edge editorial illustration work this side of New York—and are only too happy to pay you for your product or services. When you find these customers, it makes very good business sense to go out of your way to keep them.

❋ *Let the Love Flow*

Beyond the fun factor of having clients who love your work (and with whom you love to work), there is also a financial bottom line here. Clients who make your work life easy, and pay you what you are worth, are truly one of your most valuable business assets. As we touched on when we talked about word of mouth and repeat business in the marketing chapters, these clients are often not only making you money, they are saving you money in advertising and marketing costs. Generally speaking, it costs more to get a new customer than to keep an existing one.

Figuring out which of your customers are helping you achieve that magical place of profitability *and* client relation bliss will be an important part of your ongoing business plan. There is a lot of strategic value in identifying your best clients, deepening your relationship with them, and learning how to get more like them.

So how do you pick them out of the crowd? Some of them will be easy to spot: those repeat customers who are always placing web orders every time you release a new product, or the regular customers who come in every Thursday night and order the special and a nice bottle of wine. If you have a lot of customer contact, these will be the customers you love to talk to; you actually get excited when their number comes up on the call display (for real). But sometimes they'll be a little sneakier to figure out. They'll just be the clients who aren't necessarily all that noticeable, because dealing with them is so darn easy you barely notice. So, one of the other things you'll want to look at is whether or not they are making you money. If you have a service-based business, your time sheets will tell you this (more on this in Chapter 13), and if you sell a product or have a retail location you may want to go back to the customer database you build (whether it is a literal database or just a book of preferred customers) to see who the regulars are, and who is spending the most money with you.

So now that you've found them, what do you do? You may want to offer them incentives to keep coming back to shop at your store—such as frequent shopper rewards programs. You may want to let them in early on new products, because you know they'll be among the first not only to snap them up but to start spreading the word to their pals. Or you may want to give them exclusive access to sales, samples, or other bonuses. Our naturopath sends everyone a gift certificate for $20 on their birthday. While she's not discriminating between her "favorite" clients and the rest with that program, she is sending a subtle reminder to her existing client base that she's still there, and giving a deal to those clients who do come in regularly.

Loss Leaders

Typically the term "loss leader" is meant to refer to those products that are underpriced in a big retail environment to get you in the door to spend more dollars—like the super-cheap laundry soap (limit two per customer) at the drugstore. In your business it may be worth having a few loss leaders, whether they are low-priced, high-demand items that will bring some customers in the door, or (for a service-based business) a handful of clients who in some way serve you but don't necessarily measure up on the profitability end of things.

We have always been committed to maintaining a small list of clients that we either do pro bono or reduced-rate work for. We're very picky about who makes it on this list: We must love working with them, we must feel that they can otherwise not afford our services, they must very clearly understand what our services would normally cost them, and they need to understand that occasionally paying work will take precedence over them. But having this small roster of pet projects for stunning people, whom we simply adore having a chance to work with, helps keep us going during those times when we have a bunch of less inspiring, but well-paid, work.

The principle here is straightforward: If you're going to give it away, make sure you're getting something in return, and that you're giving it to your core target market—those people who are best equipped to help you bring in more star clients, or who at least make your day a little more fun.

In a service-based business like ours, we don't really have "extras" or sales to give away to our favorite clients. And often, once we've finished a big contract with a really great client, that may mean our customer won't need our website design services for a year or more. And while sometimes there is simply nothing we can do about that, when we finish a project with a really great client, we will see if there are natural ways we can continue the relationship—additional related services, maintenance, enhancements—and we make sure all our clients know how much we appreciate them by sending them gifts when their sites launch (everything from a small bouquet of flowers to bottles of champagne). Even if they can't use our services again right away, making sure they feel appreciated will help ensure that they come back to us next time they need our services—thus keeping our sales cycle healthy in the future—and in many cases lead to referrals. While there are no guarantees that your favorite clients will always send you clients just as stupendous as they are, it certainly increases your chances of getting clients who will make your workdays more pleasant.

❋ R-E-S-P-E—Okay, You Know the Rest

While sales, flowers, and giveaways are all well and lovely, they are not the only ingredients in helping you build happy customer relationships. And sometimes, let's be honest, you just can't afford to be giving too much stuff away. But while this may sound a bit Dear Abby–ish, you can always afford respect. Treating your customers with good old honest respect may seem like a no-brainer, but we continue to be blown away by how often our clients remark on it as a none-too-ubiquitous feature in some of our competitors.

Part of respect is of course just the basics of being nice, polite, and courteous with folks like your mama taught you, but we've also found that a big part of it is treating your clients as equals. Whatever you do, chances are you are doing it because you are an expert, and your customers use your products or services because of your expertise—but lording that knowledge over them just makes them feel inferior, whereas sharing your expertise with your clients helps them feel like you really value them. That's not to say that in our case we should go around teaching all our clients how to build their own websites—that wouldn't really be a sustainable business plan, nor is it what they hire us for. But, in a technical field like ours, it is very easy for us as service providers to exclude our clients with the jargon and tricks of the trade that are so second nature to us. We don't like to work that way; not only does it set up a hierarchy we aren't too comfy with, we've found that the more our clients understand what it is we are doing for them, the more they appreciate and ultimately value our work.

Client education is quite simply the process of making your clients and customers understand the value of the service or product you are offering them. And by bringing your customers up to speed, you not only help to position yourself as an expert—as in "Man, when it comes to aromatherapy and healing, that girl seriously knows her stuff"—you also help your clients feel like they aren't getting swindled by a bunch of smoke and mirrors.

Lots of businesspeople seem to be afraid of letting their customers (and the competition) peek behind the veil, and we totally understand that fear. But ultimately, you aren't giving away the whole farm, because no one is going to be able to apply the same basic facts and ingredients with the same skill, love, and dedication that you do.

CONSIDER THIS

We've always been very transparent about our website design process. We describe it on our website, and we give our clients plenty of documentation and handouts as reference material along the way. That, combined with the fact that all of our code is available for anyone to see (you can view the source on any web page to see how it is built), may make some people say we're not holding on to much in the way of our intellectual capital. And they may be right. But what if we were working hard to keep that all under wraps? Would that give us a leg up on the thousands of website designers already out there? No. What brings our clients to us is strong word of mouth generated by our solid work ethic and the special care we take with our clients. In our first few years of business, Lauren even penned an article, "Consider This," encouraging clients to reconsider just how much they needed to spend on their websites. In a time when the average website design company was trying to sell people on larger-than-life sites with the latest technology (regardless of whether or not they had a strong business case to warrant it), that article brought us all kinds of business from people who were looking for a company they felt they could trust.

❧ Promised the Moon

After respect, one of the key elements of good customer service is summed up by our favorite motto: "Underpromise; overdeliver." Whether you'll be carrying this out with a product line or a service you are going to perform, setting up reasonable customer expectations is going to make your job *so* much easier, while also keeping your customers happy.

Underpromising doesn't mean selling yourself short; it simply means being reasonable about what you commit to, and building in some contingency time for things to go slightly sideways. If you are selling a service, this can mean setting up agreed-to goals for how success will be measured at the end of the project, making sure you feel like you are going to be able to achieve those goals, and setting reasonable timelines that you actually feel give you a fair bit of breathing room. We once read some business advice that said never to commit to a timeline when you are in a client meeting; always go back to the office and take a good look at everything else you have to balance before you commit. We generally hold to that rule, or make sure we go into all client meetings with a strong sense of what is going to be achievable for us. If you are selling a product, the same theory holds true: It simply means being sure that your product is going to deliver what you claim it will. This may seem obvious—after all, you're not going to lie, right?—but sometimes it is easy to get carried away with what a client wants a product to do, and not stick to what it was really designed for. Julia Beardwood summed up the concept well when she said, "Be honest with your clients; do what you say you're going to do; don't set up unrealistic expectations; and, when you can, tell them what you really think. After all, if you can actually *overdeliver* on the expectations you've set, that's really a nice one."

We were lucky enough to have a client go out of her way to teach us this lesson. A marketing professional with years of experience managing subcontractors, she always knew an unachievable deadline when she saw one. So when she'd catch us saying things like "Great, we'll have that ready for you tomorrow," she would respond with "That's nice, but I won't have time to look at this tomorrow, and I think that is totally unrealistic. How about you have it ready for me next week?" While that may seem a bit cruel, her lesson to us (and we can't stress how valuable this was) was simply that there was no point in our breaking our necks to get something ahead of schedule. It wasn't serving anyone, and it meant we were imposing unnecessarily stressful deadlines on ourselves.

Just as you should always build contingencies into your budgets, you should also build some contingency into your timelines and deliverables. That may mean giving yourself a two-week cushion on delivering your handmade Christmas cards to your distributor—allowing for the very high likelihood of a winter flu waylaying you for a day or two—or tacking an extra fifteen minutes on to each customer appointment you make, allowing for clients to run a bit late and the phone to ring more than you would like it to. Giving yourself that breathing room not only helps you navigate waters that might get a little choppy, it also helps keep your customers happy.

❧ *The Dark Side of the Force: Firing Clients*

Okay, so the customer is always right, right? Yeah, kind of. Sometimes the customer's version of right and your version of right are not going to merge into one nice shared reality. And sometimes the cost to your business of bending over backward to make sure your customers are happy is just too high, in either the actual hard cost of what they are asking for, or simply the strain it puts on you to deal with making them happy. Some people are just plain unreasonable, and if you want to keep a handle on both your business and your sanity you need to get good at spotting them.

In your business, spotting the unreasonable cases may not be quite as easy to do as telling the lady who let her toddler throw her shoe off a cliff that no, she was not going to get a replacement (see sidebar p.209). So what should you do with the genuine customer complaints? Everyone we've spoken to who has had awkward angry-customer moments has said essentially the same thing: Kill them with kindness. It is amazing how even the seemingly angriest person can go from raging hellcat to happy kitten when you pour on the good vibes. Many folks who have a complaint—the bag they ordered didn't look the same as the photo on the website, or there's too much salt in the soup—start off angry and defensive because they aren't expecting you to care; if you show them that you do, they'll often let down their guard, opening the way for a reasonable conversation. A few of the folks we spoke to recalled irate customers who, once their issue was resolved, actually became loyal, regular customers. After all, if a business transaction goes smoothly, you're not likely to remember it, but if things go sideways and *then* the person you're dealing with goes out of her way to resolve things, that's memorable.

OH, COME ON, PEOPLE

As a teenager, Emira worked in a small specialty shoe store that sold very high-end footwear. As retailers of top-of-the-line shoes, the owners stood by their product and would always repair or replace any defects. They had a loyal customer base that was willing to pay higher prices for beautiful, comfortable shoes that were "guaranteed" to deliver quality shoe goodness. That said, there was always a string of folks who would come in demanding a replacement shoe (or shoes) for items that had fallen out of a canoe, been eaten by the family dog, left on the side of the road, dropped in a campfire, and so on. And while these people would more often than not actually freak out and leave in either a huff or a screaming fit when they were told that the policy did not indeed apply to flagrant shoe negligence, there was no way a small business could sustain making these people happy by fulfilling their requests.

It is very important that you figure out which of your customers do in fact need to be listened to and what you can filter out as the neurosis of a crazy person. While it is just as important to do what you can within your own superpowers to make customers happy, it is also just as important that you let go of the clients that are going to be nothing more than an ongoing PITA (Pain in the Ass), sucking up your valuable energy. Letting go can mean different things to different folks and levels of business. Sometimes it just means not getting too caught up in the point-by-point criticism delivered via email to your inbox, when you know you have done your best work. Other times it can actually mean taking decisive action and firing a client.

In the age of email, it seems to us like some people are only too willing to send off hate-mail tirades that they previously might not have bothered to get a stamp and envelope for. When you're running a small business and your name and reputation are on the line, it can be really hard to ignore some of those crazy, negative emails. We know a few gals who have purposely set things up so that a staff person reads their customer complaint emails. That staff person has to be well trained to know when things should indeed be passed up the chain to the boss to handle, but it means the owners no longer have to cope with the emotional trauma of reading some of the abuse that folks send to their inboxes. Of those who don't have staff, some set all those emails aside to deal with them in a chunk once a week/month so that they can fortify themselves mentally to wade through the abuse and deal with the genuine issues. That way, they don't get derailed by their emotions while trying to get other things done. Scheduling a cocktail with a friend or a kickboxing class for after those times isn't a bad idea either.

Now, in the rules that govern a market economy, you can't ultimately prevent a customer from coming into your restaurant, buying your stuff, or using your services, but you can do your best to end your relationship when you suspect it really isn't serving you anymore. In some ways, it can be a bit easier for consultants than it is for those of you with a storefront—unless you want to hire some muscle to redirect the undesirable customer of note—to take action to end the relationship. That said, when you are dealing with larger contracts it can be really hard to say no to repeat work or to walk away from an existing contract.

The first time we had to fire a client it tore us up. The whole process from start to finish was a nightmare, which really only ended when we finally made the decision to let the project go. Here's how it went down:

We were about fourteen months into our business, and had just landed a project whose budget was almost as large as our entire income from the past year. We were over the moon. We had initial project meetings, got the project started, and then started to get worried. The clients had very unreasonable expectations. They wanted us to build them a website that would fix some of the problems inherent in their overall operating plan (but were unwilling to address those problems at all).

We tried to be very clear about separating the goals of the project from the overall goals they needed to address in their organization, and tried to set some targets for measuring the success of *this* project. They resisted. We started to seriously fret. We felt like it would be totally unprofessional to walk away from a project that had started; we would not only have to lose the final payment but perhaps refund some of the money we had already received—and to make matters worse, we had turned down some work in order to focus on this large contract. We felt totally stuck. And as the days went by, we felt more and more uneasy.

Then, the clients began to take unreasonable to new and bizarre places: leaving us angry, yelling voice mail when we weren't available at all hours of the day, doubting our skill set after we had been very clear about the scope of work that we were going to perform and what our process to complete it would be. We began to actually feel sick about the entire project. And finally, about three weeks into the project, we decided it wasn't worth it. No matter how much we were going to get paid for this project, it was not enough to make it worth the stress and trauma it was bringing us.

So after evaluating what would actually happen if we let go of the contract—the company would go into debt until we could replace the work; we would have to face the clients' chastisement—we decided to take the leap and called the clients to negotiate terms to end our relationship. By the time that phone call was over, we felt like we had won the lottery. Sure, we were walking a financial tightrope, and would still have to pay for that fancy celebration dinner we had when we first got the contract, but—and this will sound very cheesy—we had our joy back. Over the few weeks we had been involved in the project, those clients had managed to turn our beloved company into an intensely stressful chore.

(The really happy ending to this story is that not twenty-four hours later we had a phone call from a new client, and soon found ourselves booked up with work that we really enjoyed doing—and that we would have had to turn down to focus on the other, larger, stressful project.)

As we say, the situation will be a bit different for you if you have a retail store or make a product, but the principles will be largely the same. If you find you have customers that simply do not appreciate what you offer, find subtle (or not-so-subtle) ways to direct them elsewhere—somewhere where both of you will be happier.

❀ *It's Not You—It's Me*

Sometimes you won't need to fire customers because they are sinister twits that will never be happy; sometimes it will be because they are standing in the way of your success or growth. In those cases, letting go of customers is a part of the bigger picture in customer service, as it frees up your time to deal with the customers you do love.

How could paying customers possibly be standing in the way of your success, you ask? If they are no longer a good fit for your company. As your business grows and evolves, it is likely to change in subtle and sometimes major ways. You may start to target your marketing at slightly different audiences, as you get a better sense of just who your customer really is. You may raise your fees as your competencies increase (more on raising your fees in Chapter 14 as you think about expanding your business), and you may decide to start focusing more narrowly on one aspect of your business that is proving to be more profitable. Often these shifts in your business will happen in ways that feel natural and small at the time, but after a while you may find that some of your existing customer base doesn't really fit into your current target audience. And while sometimes that is fine, it can be a good practice to sit down once a year or so (we've started doing this at our annual year-end review meeting) and evaluate whether or not there are clients or sets of customers you need to initiate a breakup with.

As a small business, we know most of our customers quite well, and to be honest, this process can be kind of tricky. We truly adore a large section of our client base, and often we become quite interested and personally invested in their business or organization, so saying goodbye can actually be quite tough. However, we have found this process to be beneficial to everyone involved. And while that may sound very much like something a couples counselor would say, it is often true. Often, if a relationship with a client isn't working for you, for whatever reason, the same is likely true for them.

❀ *You're Holding Me Back*

One challenge that seems to plague all kinds of business, but hits retailers and manufacturers of a product the most, is cash flow. And when it comes to manufacturing your own goods and then selling them wholesale to others, cash flow can actually sometimes be a reason to let go of a client. (We'll get into the details of managing cash flow in the next chapter, on money.)

Obviously if your clients are not paying their bills, you are not going to continue to do business with them. But what if they just aren't paying on time? Like really not on time? When your business model requires that you lay out the cash to produce your product, put in all the work, ship it, and then start all over again while waiting to get paid, you often can't afford to sit around on invoices for too long. And in some cases, long delays in payment are a solid reason to let a customer go. Unfortunately, we have seen this happen when small manufacturers start selling to larger retailers or get really big contracts, which is so very lame because many of us dream of having our goods on the shelves of larger retailers, where the logic tells us we'll sell more. And while that may be true, if those big retailers are causing you to have to finance major production runs while you then wait around forever to be paid, then sometimes it really isn't worth it. Ditto for smaller companies who are slow as molasses on the accounts payable front. (Those ones are just a bit easier to let go of.)

❀ *Coming Back for More*

Customer service may seem like a bit of a no-brainer; after all, no one starts a business with the goal of alienating friends, family, and perfect strangers, but you can never underestimate the value of customer satisfaction in maintaining the health of your business as it grows. Whether they are retail customers or service-based clients, maintaining and building good relationships with your customers will not only make your job more pleasant, it will help to bring in more customers and spread good word throughout the community about your business. Happy customers can act like unpaid sales staff, finding you more of the best customers and sending them your way—meaning less (and more-enjoyable) work for you.

And when things go wrong, don't hesitate to turn away customers who just can't be satisfied. Trust your gut; if it tells you they aren't a good fit for you, then let them know you've got a great tip for them— it's a great little shop just down the street. . . .

CHAPTER 13

Financial Reality Check

(a.k.a. Money, Again)

THAT'S RIGHT: IT'S TIME to talk money, again. We discussed some money basics, such as planning your start-up budget and business finances, early on in Chapter 3, and we're coming back to it now as we look at maintaining your business. We are certainly not the kinds of gals who think that money makes the world go round, but money is a big piece of maintaining and growing your business. Just as those beeping machines next to hospital beds monitor patients' vital signs, your finances tell the story of your business's health. Whether you've been up and running for one month or twelve, you need to track your financials so you can measure how you're doing.

If you're the type who'd rather do almost anything than read financial statements, maybe you need to get a handle on just how those numbers relate to your daily life—and not just in the sense of "money = good," because we all know things aren't that simple.

Your financial statements are aptly named, because they're the *statements* that answer your money *questions*. Questions like, How come I'm working my butt off and I'm still carrying a credit card balance? Where did all that money from that huge sale go? And are there money cycles I should be aware of for future planning?

Before we go any further, we should get one thing clear: We aren't going to teach you how to read your financial statements. That's a topic for a whole other book (of which there are many), and frankly, we're no substitute for a good accountant. What we will do is run down the bits and pieces of financial wisdom we've found most helpful, and give you some tips on where (and when) to find more assistance.

❀ *Putting Your Budget to the Test*

Here's a fun accounting term to start us off: budget vs. actual. You can probably figure that one out on your own, but all we're talking about here is taking that lovely budget you put together back in Chapter 3 and holding it up to the light to make sure you're on track. The "budget" part you should already have; the "actual" requires you (or your bookkeeper) to calculate what you've *actually* spent and earned to date. If you've got yourself set up with an accounting program (and you've kept all your receipt entries up to date), getting a snapshot of your actual expenses to date will be a breeze. And if you happen to be the kind of gal who likes to get into the nitty-gritty number crunching, then this will be like having your very own ticker tape parade! The report you are looking for here is an income and expense report, which will list out all of your expenses to date in handy categories like "Transportation," "Meals and Entertainment," and so on. You can ask your bookkeeper for this report, generate it yourself in QuickBooks/ Simply Accounting—or if you've got a pile of spreadsheets or ledger books, do a bit of math yourself.

The goal here is pretty simple: Have a look at each item and see where you're ahead and where you're behind. If you're like most of us, you'll be ahead in expenses and behind in income. If that describes you, don't panic. It's totally normal. After all, none of us have crystal balls when we're developing our initial budgets, and especially in your first few years, estimating your expenses for any particular category is an educated guess at best. Reviewing these reports as you plan for future years will help you get closer to the mark, but there will likely always be unexpected expenses and fluctuations to keep you on your toes.

Now, let's try and get more specific about what you're looking at here: If expenses are higher than you'd projected, see if you can pinpoint the items that are pushing you over. Did you wildly underestimate your software costs (likely to be a once-every-couple-of-years type of expense), or are you simply having to lay out more cash for inventory because your products are flying off the shelves (which is a great problem to have)? The things to note are whether these higher-than-expected costs are likely to be ongoing, or just one-time deals. If you expect them to recur from month to month, you should probably amend your budget to reflect your new, more accurate costs of doing business.

Of course, it should go without saying that if your expenses are high because you've been spending money on things in the "gravy" column while your revenues are barely keeping your head above water, now is the time to start reining yourself in. That beautiful stationery and those lovely celebration lunches may need to wait until you're established and standing on firmer financial ground.

❧ *Something Still Doesn't Add Up*

What if you review your costs and your sales, and everything is pretty much where you expected it to be when you started out, but you still find you're working way more than you expected and not seeing your bank balance grow as much as you'd like? You probably didn't account for how long it would take you to do things, or how much extra work goes into running a business.

> When we spoke to Cinnamon Cooper of Poise bags, she said that it wasn't so much the cost of goods that she had underestimated when she started out as how much time "running the business" would actually take. "I really underestimated how much it would cost to do everything from filing to answering customer emails to sourcing new fabrics." Now instead of answering every email question she gets, she tries to address similar types of questions on her business blog, and she had to raise the prices for her bags to account for all the time that went into just managing Poise.

If you're in the happy position of having higher expenses because your revenue is also way off the projected chart, then it's time to think about treating yourself to something on your wish list. If you are doing more business than you had planned to, you will of course have higher expenses, so we don't want you getting all worried about that.

What should you do if your revenues are low? Aside from digging around in the couch cushions for spare change, and searching your pockets for that winning lottery ticket, we have some concrete suggestions to help sort things out—and we'll get to those in a minute. For now, though, try again to sort out whether this is likely to be an ongoing issue, so that you can revise your budget if necessary. We don't want you dreading your budget vs. actual every time, after all. Better to plug in some more achievable figures so you aren't disappointed when you fail to reach the more ambitious original ones.

If you're on or under budget, congratulations! Either you know yourself very well, or you've done this kind of thing before. (Or, like us, you count yourself among the world's more pessimistic money planners and budgeted for high contingencies.) But there are more pieces to the money puzzle beyond your budget ... like profitability.

If your business is particularly new (as in less than six months old), it may be difficult to determine whether your current financial state is evidence of things to come. In this case, you may need to wait a bit longer before revising your budget or making any drastic changes—but it's still important to run through your budget vs. actual to make sure there aren't any major surprises. You wouldn't want to go six months without noticing your landlord is overcharging you on rent.

❋ *Profiting from Your Efforts*

Once you have a strong handle on how much cash has come into (and gone out of) your business, you can turn your attention to the question of profit. We know that for some of you, the word "profit" conjures up images of oil execs taking off into the night with other people's cash, but here we're simply talking about what's left over when you've paid your bills. Think of profit as your business's own savings account; it's the "gravy" money that gets reinvested into the business, so that you can progress from your "no-frills" budget to your dreamland scenario.

Profits will help you:

- stabilize your cash flow by helping tide you over in rough patches;

- invest in better equipment, more inventory, or product development;

- give yourself a raise;

- hire staff and/or freelance assistance (such as an accountant, lawyer, business coach, or—ahem—website designer);

- give employees bonuses either as one-offs or in the form of profit-sharing agreements, where you split up the profits with them based on a percentage system;

- donate to your favorite charities—we talked to a lot of women who donate a percentage of their profits as a part of their regular business plan;

- start in on your wish list, whether it's to send yourself on a creative retreat or move into a new space.

In other words, profit is what's going to take you beyond your start-up scenario and into the future. So we need to figure out how to get you profitable.

The first step toward determining how profitable you are is already complete: You've reviewed your income and expenses, compared them to your budget, and assessed whether or not you're on track. Since we're pretty sure your budget was a balanced one, you can consider yourself profitable so long as you're on or under budget.

However, if you're among the 90 percent of businesses whose budget does not reflect the precise nature of reality, you'll need to look at some additional measures.

For instance, say you sold out of your stock of handmade greeting cards within your first two weeks, when you had expected them to last two months. As a result, you had to spend a bunch of money on materials to replenish your shelves—and it's thrown off your whole budget.

That type of cash outlay is not only common—it's a testament to your success. The only trick here is making sure you're earning enough to keep some spare change in the bank for occasions like these. Because chances are, next time you'll be spending even more, and your investment in materials will continue to grow as your customer base expands.

The key elements to keep an eye on in your budget are cost of goods—you'll want to make sure that stays pretty constant so that your prices continue to work for you—and your other ongoing expenses such as overhead and payroll. If your basic, month-to-month expenses are on track, and your productivity is good (i.e., you aren't spending twice as long to make each card as you expected), your profits should be healthy.

❧ *Woman of the Hour*

Now, if you're an hourly-rate type—a consultant, that is—your key profit measure is your time sheets. You'll need to add up the time you've spent on each project, and compare that to the income you gained from those clients. Even if you haven't yet completed a project, you should have a solid sense of where your budget is, so you can make informed decisions as you go. (We update our time sheet totals weekly.)

You may be on budget, but only because you've been working seventy-hour weeks, and essentially giving away your time to demanding clients. The goal here is to have you reach all the aims of your original plan, so if you're consistently hitting 150 percent of budget by the time a project's complete, you know it's time to adjust your project estimates accordingly.

You can learn a few other interesting things from time sheets, such as which clients are sucking you dry. (They're the ones whose budgets, no matter how high, fall by the wayside early on, never to recover.) You can also find the projects that consistently come in *under* budget, and those are the ones you want more of, because they'll keep you afloat in the long run.

It's always a challenge to take a cold, hard look at the numbers, because you may well see that your favorite clients are the ones monopolizing your time. And that may be because you're indulging them out of affection, which is perfectly fine—so long as it isn't costing your business time and money. But when their demands begin to compromise your fiscal health (or your ability to leave the office), it's time to sit them down and have a frank discussion about what's working and what isn't. And while it's generally bad practice to try to renegotiate pricing after the fact (unless the scope of work has changed), you may need to remind them of the parameters you agreed to so that you're not bending over backward *and* losing money.

More importantly, the process of evaluating your project-by-project profits will help you plan for the future. You'll have a better grasp of what types of projects make you money, and which ones are sure losers. Honing that spidey-sense will be invaluable in helping you suss out prospective clients.

While you may think that in your early stages, any client's a good client, we've found that belief to be false. If you have an inkling that you're going to lose money on a project, consider that you stand to lose not only in financial terms—you'll also have committed yourself to something that takes you away from other prospective work. And your frustration at being underpaid is likely to rub off on your performance as well, which could lead to a less-than-stellar end result.

When you're starting out, you're establishing not only your financial base but also your reputation. Consider each project as a partnership, and ask yourself whether this client is going to bring you additional work you'll enjoy (and profit from), and if you're both likely to end up satisfied with the final product. Some clients are worth taking a financial risk for, but in many cases it's better to walk away from a bad deal ahead of time and save yourself some grief down the road.

❀ *Hustle and Flow*

If your financial statements are cardiac charts, your cash flow is the blood in your veins. During your first year of business, you'll see cash coming and going through your bank account at a rate you may never have imagined possible. As soon as one bill is paid, another arrives—and meanwhile, your invoices are all past due and there's no sign of a check in the mail.

The term for all this movement of money through your business is cash flow, and while the idea of "cash flowing" may seem very appealing, the struggle with cash flow is one thing that almost all businesses seem to have in common at one time or another. Just say "cash flow" in a group of even the most successful businesspeople you know, and we guarantee that eyes will roll and groans will follow. Cash flow is the art of balancing your income and expenses from day to day, so that the latter never gets too far ahead of the former, and if you can find a way to navigate your own cash flow gracefully, you'll make your business life that much easier.

Your bank account may give you the most accurate monthly cash flow report in your first year, so you can start there if you aren't yet set up with accounting software or a bookkeeper. (These last two will be able to break the report down into helpful categories, but unless you're a retailer with several product lines, you can probably get by with a bank statement for a while.)

Chances are, many of your expenses will hit on the first of the month: rent and paychecks, which compose two major chunks of outgoing cash, for starters. So you may want to start there, and compare your first-of-the-month balances over a period of several months. Do you notice any patterns? Perhaps you're consistently dipping into your overdraft to cover those checks, or maybe you see a steady climb (or decrease). It could be that there's no discernible pattern, and that's perfectly fine, too—although if your balance is fluctuating wildly between the extremes of solvency and heavy debt, that's something to make a note of, too.

For most young businesses, the challenge is how to even out cash flow, so that you're not scrambling each month to pay the bills. Here are some of the lessons we've learned over the years.

❧ Bringing Up the Arrears

The quickest way to drum up some much-needed cash is to keep on top of your accounts receivable (AR)—in other words, all those folks who owe you money. For retailers, this may mean negotiating with your payment processors so that you get your credit card purchase money more promptly; for consultants, it often entails going through your past-due invoices and giving your clients a friendly reminder that their account is outstanding. (For those of you averse to this, it may help to know that we often discover upon phoning past-due clients that they've actually misplaced the invoice and are grateful for the reminder. Of course there are always the unfortunate exceptions, but we've had a good track record of being paid.)

If you make your living from invoiced work and are struggling with cash flow problems, you may want to consider changing your payment terms so that they work better for you. This may be as simple as changing your terms from being due within thirty days to fourteen, or it may mean revising your payment structure. Four years into Raised Eyebrow's existence, we changed from a 50/50 system (50 percent as a deposit and 50 percent upon completion) to a 50/25/25 one, where clients were billed at a mutually agreed-upon, interim stage. Not only did this help us get our bank balance in better shape but it also provided our clients with much-needed incentive to keep the project moving at a time when many of them are tempted to let other priorities distract them.

> *Most of us don't fancy ourselves as collections agents, and the idea of calling up a client to ask for our money feels a bit distasteful. Well, it's time to get over that. For starters, many people simply forget about their bills and need a reminder—so it's a good idea to start out by assuming they're in that group.*
>
> *Past-due invoices can wreak serious havoc with your business's finances, so try to set aside time every two weeks to go through your invoices and call up anyone who's behind schedule. (You may want to write down the dates you called, so you have a record for future reference.)*
>
> *If you find that after several tries, there are one or two invoices that just aren't getting paid, you have several options: You can keep trying; you can call your lawyer and see if a brusque letter does the trick (or, failing that, small claims court); you can bring in a freelance collections agent; or you can write off the money as "bad debt" (which we've done a couple of times for invoices that are too small to bother paying lawyer's fees or an agent's percentage).*

❀ Can You Credit It?

Although it can be a struggle to get credit as a fledgling business, one of the most useful financial tools we have is our line of credit at the bank. At first we were a bit wary about going into too much debt for the business, but time and time again we found ourselves stressed out as the month came to an end (because first-of-the-month bills were just around the corner) and we didn't have the dollars in the bank to meet payroll, rent, and other basic expenses—even though we had a stack of accounts receivable just waiting to be paid and were working our buns off. In situations like these, or for businesses that make a product and therefore need to spend money to make any money, a line of credit may be the only way to actually keep your business ticking. For our own needs, we applied for credit in the amount of approximately one month's expenses, and it has helped us a great deal in managing the up-and-down nature of small business cash flow.

TAKING SOME CREDIT

We covered this in Chapter 3 when you were looking at financing the early days of your business, but as your business grows, you'll still run up against a need for cash. So should you take out a line of credit, get a loan, or max out your credit cards? All are viable options for financing business growth, but don't just lean on the first credit that comes your way without evaluating the pros and cons of each. Credit cards are by far the easiest form of credit to come across these days, and we spoke to more than one business gal who said she had a very comfy relationship with her credit card—Jen LaBelle of Romp pays for as much as she can with her Amex card, as it's like giving herself thirty days to pay on everything—but don't forget how high those interest charges are. If you don't expect to pay your credit off for a while, see about getting a line of credit or a business loan.

If you have personal credit available, you can use that in cases where you need to miss a paycheck, but it's easier and smarter to keep your business and personal finances separate if possible. After all, you may need to dig into your personal line of credit one day when your trusty '84 VW van starts making not-so-happy ticking noises on the way to work.

❄ The Big Hump

Some businesses, especially retailers and product-based companies, suffer from "big hump" syndrome: Most of their business happens in big chunks. Many retailers can do more business in the eight weeks leading up to Christmas than in the rest of the year combined. Those creating and selling a product will often have similar boom-and-bust episodes around trade shows, craft fairs, or fashion seasons. The trick to navigating these financial roller coasters is easy to say, and hard to do: Save carefully. When an influx of cash arrives, be prepared to make it last until the next "hump time."

If you find it simply too tempting to have that big pile of cash in the bank, try this: Write post-dated checks for all the expenses you already know are coming up: rent, insurance, paychecks, tax, and so on. Write enough to last you until your next expected windfall. Or keep all that surplus cash in an entirely separate account that is maybe just a little bit harder to get at—you may even be able to earn a small stash of interest off the money if you can keep it in a high-interest savings account or short-term investment like a GIC (guaranteed investment certificate)—then you can transfer funds into your checking account to pay the bills and keep things running each month.

Once you've entered all your checks into your books, you'll get a much more realistic picture of what that big chunk of money is actually going to do for you. Total everything up, set it against your large-and-lovely bank balance, and see if you have any extra. (If so, congratulations! You are free to spend as you wish.)

> *You are remembering what we said about keeping your tax money aside, aren't you? If that detail slipped your mind in the first couple of months, now's the time to play catch-up. You really don't want to get hit with a humongous tax bill next year, do you? Few things suck harder than seeing your dearly earned cash gobbled up in one big mouthful by the tax beast. Small, regular payments into a special savings account are just so much less painful.*

> *By the way, the same goes for any sales tax you collect through your business. Every tax penny you get from your customers goes straight to the bureaucrats, so save yourself the headache later and get your ducks in a row now.*

❈ Making Smart Purchases

If your expenses are running away with you, you may need to develop a purchase plan. In essence, this goes back to the stuff we talked about in Chapter 3: dividing your expenses into "negotiable" and "non-negotiable." The latter will obviously need to get paid no matter what, but the former should be prioritized based on your current cash situation. What you may want to do is set yourself a reward system; for example, you might decide that if you manage to carry a $1,000+ balance in your bank account for thirty days, you get to upgrade to a new printer.

The same tactic can be used for ongoing expenses. If you're having trouble determining when to upgrade to that new office space, let your cash flow be the guide. Unless your bank balance is climbing steadily, you probably don't have enough consistent income to warrant an increase in your monthly expenses. But if you find you've had three to six months of surpluses, you're probably in good shape to move on up.

It can also be helpful to prioritize your wish list, so that you don't make snap purchasing decisions based on whatever seems most urgent at the time. Step back with a clear mind and run down your list of "nonnegotiables." Which are the most strategically important for the business? Are there some that are likely to increase your revenues? Will any of them bring in new clientele, or increase satisfaction levels for your existing customers? Those go to the top of the list. And the purely fun ones can move down. (Although if there's a $50 gizmo that would make you incredibly happy every time you go to work, well hey—who are we to say no to you?)

✿ *Money: Helping You Get a Good Night's Sleep*

Keeping a close eye on your business finances isn't everyone's idea of fun, but it's a bit like checking the foundation of your house: You want to make sure everything's in order there before you jump into decorating and building an addition. If it doesn't come naturally to you, don't fret—you're not alone. Many of us jump into self-employment with only the foggiest idea of what "accounts payable" means. And while continually going back to your finances to see what's happening may sound like it will lead you to dreams filled with dollar signs and spreadsheets, the idea here is not to become obsessed with money, in fact just the opposite. By staying on top of your finances, and making sure your business is running at a level to take care of your financial needs, you can start to forget about the details and get on with the work that you love.

Of course, even with two chapters on the topic, we've barely scratched the surface of the world of finances. If you're feeling up to a little more reading, check out our resources section for book and website recommendations. After all, you could write a whole book on this stuff—and as it turns out, many people have.

And as we've mentioned a few times before, your accountant or bookkeeper is your closest ally on this stuff. Don't be afraid to ask questions, and call on them for advice; that's what they're there for.

Finally, try to make a regular date with yourself to review your finances. The more time you spend with them, the more familiar you'll become with the figures that matter most for your business, and the better you'll understand the impact of some of the suggestions we've made in this chapter. Even a half-hour check-in will do you a world of good. There's nothing like understanding money talk to boost your confidence—particularly at those industry events where people are always bragging about their sales figures. (You'll start to see that those folks who go on and on about their "$1 million in sales last year" rarely speak about their *profits* . . . and suddenly their big-shot talk doesn't seem quite so intimidating.) Besides, you're going to need a bit of spare cash to get through the hurdles in the next chapter: expanding, oh my!

CHAPTER 14

Expanding

First off, several serious rounds of huzzah for you! If you're starting to think about growing your business—hiring staff, expanding your services/products, opening your own storefront, etc.—then you deserve some serious praise. Getting here is no piece of cake; we know well all the work it has taken to get here and wish to congratulate you from the very bottom of our hearts. (For more on celebrating your success, read on to Chapter 15.)

Some of you may have been planning this since the very beginning, anxiously waiting for the day when you could move your home office out of your bedroom and into a groovy little office space with a view, budgeting for the day you make the big leap from blogging about your wares to actually opening your own online storefront, or slogging through the grind of being the only one there to mind the shop until you could afford to pay an employee or two. If that's the case, then taking this step may be a bit easier for you, mentally speaking, than for others who may have dug in their heels, vehemently insisting that staying small was their raison d'être. Sound like we're speaking from experience? That would be because we are.

We've already talked about how this book is not a typical business book; it is not aimed at starting a business with an eye to making quick cash, or making it big all fast and furious like. One of our big motivators for writing this book was that we felt there were too few books out there that reinforced the idea that it is okay to stay small—to build your own business that takes care of you and maybe a few employees, and that allows you to do something that you love while getting paid what you are worth. And frankly, we reacted pretty strongly against all the hype—which is particularly bad when you're in anything related to computers and the Internet—that can fill your head as people you meet start telling you about how you should take big leaps forward in the service of making yourself a quick buck. But here's the big lesson we want to pass on: Small doesn't mean stuck. You can grow in all kinds of ways that work for you and your business regardless of what those guys on late-night TV say about making fast cash with their proven system.

In the early days of Raised Eyebrow, we knew this one guy who was forever proclaiming, "If you're not growing, you're dying," every single time we saw him. And saying that to two headstrong gals, who had founded their business on the principle that small was beautiful, kind of got our panties in a twist. (Kind of a lot actually.) "What is that all about?!" we would wail. "Why must we 'grow, grow, grow'? Is it not enough to just want to build our business one client at a time and get paid what we're worth?" And for years, we kept along our path of growing at a reasonable pace, staying out of debt and incrementally raising both our rates and our salaries as our client base grew with us. We regularly declared that particular dude to be "so very off base"— and in some ways we were right, but in others (while it pains us to admit it), we were missing out on the larger lesson. While the vision of hiring scads of staff (which we knew we could not support) and expanding to offshore development to keep our rates competitive— resulting in our paying other people what we would never consider a living wage so that we could make some cash off their backs—was in no way in line with our business model or personal values, that didn't mean that some growth wasn't necessary to keep our business healthy and us happy.

In this chapter we're going to talk about different ways of growing, how to figure out when you might be ready for growth, and how to make sure you grow in ways that stay true to your vision of what your business should look like. So whether you're thinking two years down the road or ready to take the plunge now, it's time to take a few minutes to think about what kind of growth is going to keep your business in its happy place.

GO TEAM?

So how did we make the leap from being vehemently against growth to taking on staff and doing all kinds of scary growing stuff? As we mentioned back in Chapter 11, we hired a business coach. So just what is a business coach? Do they set up your playbook and hand you water at halftime? Not exactly. Business coaches do help push you to do your best, though. A business coach will work with you to help you outline the big-picture, long-term, and short-term goals for your business, and then will help you set up plans to achieve those goals. What does that actually look like? Well for us, it means taking some focused time out of our days—usually once every six to eight weeks—to sit down with someone who helps us shift out of our regular "to-do list" brains and think more strategically about why we became entrepreneurs in the first place and plan for the years ahead.

❀ Buzz Kill

If there is one word that is particularly overused these days (particularly out here on the oh-so-eco-friendly West Coast), it's "sustainable." While this term seems to get thrown around by everyone from politicians to those folks who write the marketing copy on the back of your cane-juice-sweetened spelt flake breakfast cereal, what does it actually mean when it comes to your business? While we'd love to encourage you to develop your business in ways that leave as positive an impact as possible on the environment—we are from the West Coast, after all—we're not talking about environmentally friendly growth here particularly. The principles are pretty much the same, though. We are talking about making sure you expand your business in ways that you can manage and that don't cause total destruction of your business's healthy habitat. That means taking small steps (or big ones when you know you're ready) from a position of educated knowledge about what both you and your business can handle, and most importantly in ways that you know your business can support.

Growing sustainably is really just about making sure that you have the resources to sustain the growth you initiate, whether that is enough hours in a day to take on more work, enough money to pay employees to help you take on more work, or enough expertise in-house to deal with new challenges. Evaluating your internal resources—money, skill sets, hours in the day, space in the store—before you initiate new growth will help you ensure that your expansion will be sustainable.

❀ Risky Business

One of the big reasons that we were always squeamish about "big growth" for our business was our fear of taking big risks. While we are obviously not entirely risk averse—after all, like you, we started our own business, and just taking that step rather than getting another predictable paying job contains a certain level of risk—we were pretty happy maintaining that one level of risk that we had become comfortable with. For example, by not hiring any employees in our early years, we were avoiding the risk of not being able to pay someone's paycheck; we remained responsible for our own incomes only. The stats show that as business*women* we were not alone in this. Women-owned businesses tend to be viewed as generally lower-risk investments by those folks at the bank who lend money, and the conventional wisdom is that women take fewer risks with their money. (You may want to remind them of that if you are having trouble being taken seriously.) And generally we have to admit we're all about taking the "safer" routes to achievable success, rather than setting ourselves up for a big fall. While part of our sticking to what feels comfortable has to do with some squeamishness around taking big risks, our guiding principle is simply a desire to be conscious of and careful about the risks we do take so that we don't end up unnecessarily putting our business in harm's way.

That said, risks (like taxes) are inevitable even in the most solid of business plans, and when you're looking at expanding, you're always going to be evaluating your comfort zone. Some growth and change are going to be necessary to keep your business healthy, and that is always going to involve some degree of risk. So take a deep breath (unless of course downhill mountain biking is your favorite hobby and risk is already your middle name), and take a look at what kinds of risk are going to help you expand your business while still allowing you to sleep at night. And so, with a solid picture of your current finances in hand (you did that back in Chapter 13, remember), we're going to walk you through some different growth scenarios that life as an entrepreneur may bring your way—everything from figuring out what to do with all your profit (that's the easy one), to figuring out where you'll get the extra cash to expand your horizons.

YOU, INC.

While we're not going to delve too far into the business of in-corporation vs. partnerships and sole proprietors—we touched on this before back in Chapter 4, and we do urge you to talk to your local government-run small business branch, a lawyer, and/or your accountant on this one—we want to bring it up again here. Aside from changing how you do your taxes and what it says on your checks, incorporation is primarily about mitigating risk. As a sole proprietor or partnership, the risks your business takes are, financially and legally, squarely on your shoulders. As an incor-porated business, you can have some separation between your personal and business risks. So as you expand your business and increase/change the levels of risk you are facing, you'll want to check in with those experts to see whether or not you've reached a point where it is worth taking the legal step to becoming an official incorporated business. Don't worry—it isn't totally icky, and it al-lows you to introduce yourself as "the man" at your high school reunion. (Kidding.)

❇ Heavens, Whatever Will I Do with All This Extra Money?

Okay, so this ranks numero uno as the very best business growth "prob-lem" to be facing—hands down. That said, whether you've got an ex-tra two hundred bucks or two thousand at the end of the month/year, you need to decide what to do with it. Back in the finances chapter, we talked about budgeting to reinvest money back into the company, and while we would positively love it if all your budgeting dreams always came true, honestly that has been one of the line items in our own budgets that often go by the wayside come year-end, for while we manage to meet all our other targets and stay largely out of debt, this one seems tricky to attain. However, in the happy circumstance that you do have extra cash on hand, what do you do with it?

As we outlined back in Chapter 13, reinvesting in your business is kind of like building up a company savings account. Once you've got a healthy savings balance, you can think about how you want to spend it. And chances are, after you've done some visioning exercises at the company staff retreat, you'll want to spend it on all this fabulous growth and expansion.

Those funds can get reinvested in helping you bridge to the next level in higher operating expenses—higher salaries, more salaries, bigger rent, new computers/sewing machines/tattoo guns/etc.—or you may actually wish to make investments as a company. Just as you can put your own cash in things like buying a house, which serves the dual roles of keeping a roof over your head and likely (given general real estate trends) generating some more money if and when you sell, so can your business. If you have the capital (i.e., cashola) to start making investments in the name of your business, then it is certainly worth thinking about that. But because these will be big money transactions, you should really get your well-heeled self to some kind of financial advisor and have a chat with those folks who take care of your taxes to see what taking these steps will mean for you.

UMM . . . CAN I BORROW A DIME?

So what happens if you need to grow and you don't have all that nice extra cash lying around, huh? Good question—and before we answer, we'd like to note that you are not alone. Frankly, this is the position most of us find ourselves in at least a few times in the life of our business. And often a cash flow crunch will be a direct result of growing/expanding. These are times when you need to get an outside cash injection to get you to the next level, whether it's in the form of an investment from a family member or friend, or a bank loan. For more on growth and cash flow, keep reading.

❀ Cloning Is Not an Option

Do you find yourself daydreaming about building a robot "you" who could help you double your productivity (and sleep time!), so that you can begin to climb out from under all the things piling up on your to-do list? Time to hire some staff. We took you through some evaluation tools for when it is time to hire in Chapter 11, but we want to bring it up briefly again here.

> ### RAISE YOUR RATES!
>
> *Here's a scenario that's become so familiar we've considered having T-shirts made. A girlfriend who is a few years into her new business meets us for a drink to talk shop. After regaling us with all her recent successes, she sighs and says, "Yeah, it's great. But I'm so tired. I'd love some help, but I just can't afford it." At this point we will generally shout over one another with a forceful "Raise your prices!" While we'd like to take the credit for this basic but often-overlooked piece of wisdom, it came into our lives through Emira's grandpa Jack. Every time she went home to see him and told him about our full roster of clients, he would congratulate her success and counsel her to raise her rates to finance the expenses that success ultimately brings. If you're so busy that it's a problem and you still can't afford to hire someone, then it's time to raise your rates. You may lose a few customers, but you'll increase your income and save your sanity.*

In addition to helping you deal with the work at hand, hiring staff should pay for itself—really. While you should be relatively certain before you hire staff that you are going to have the income to keep them on the payroll, you should also look at whether or not that staff is going to help your business make money. For a service- or consultancy-based business like ours, that means making sure that staff person will be able to fill enough of their time with billable client work. For those of you making a product, that staff person should enable you to increase your production run and/or speed it up enough that you can meet targets and deliver your lovely goods to customers on time. If you're running a storefront kind of business, your staff should allow you valuable time away from the daily grind for days off (very important) and big-picture business thinking that will be invaluable in sustaining your shop.

❁ *Moving On Up*

In the first months of 2000, right before the dot-com bubble took its oh-so-inevitable hit, we set up offices in the corner of Lauren's bedroom. These were days when our colleagues were working out of chic office spaces with foosball tables, pop machines, and "chill rooms," so you could say that we were kind of bucking the trend. We had our two computers set up in the cozy corner, sharing a single dial-up Internet connection, and with those resources we made it through our first few website launches and contracts. About a year later, we moved into taking over half the living room when Lauren's honey moved in (making the bedroom a little more crowded). From there we got shared office space in a heritage office building in an eclectic downtown neighborhood (eclectic = cheap rent), and somewhere near our four-year mark we took that space over completely. Each of these moves coincided with what we needed at the time. And while we can't complain about our current budget ocean and mountain views, we do dream of one day having more space and possibly a change of scenery.

While it's all well and good to pinch pennies on your overhead, if your business can sustain writing bigger rent checks for swankier space (and it makes good business sense to have it, or it will simply make you extremely happy), then rent a U-Haul: It is time to move on up. It may also be that you don't so much move up as start replicating yourself. Take our example of Smoking Lily and their too lovely "smallest retail outlet in Canada" shop in Victoria, B.C. When they found themselves in a comfy financial place and feeling like they were firmly established at a size they wanted to maintain—but couldn't see expanding in the Victoria market—they decided to spread their wings out to the mainland and set up a second shop in Vancouver. They could afford a bigger location at their home base, but why mess with a good thing? The expansion was made with the help of a good friend and longtime employee who wanted to move to the big smoke around the same time.

More/bigger/better space for your business will often come knocking on your door before you have a chance to start thinking about it, whether it is because you have more staff/stock than can fit in your current locale, or because you suddenly find yourself spending way too many hours commuting back and forth to client meetings all day and need a more central home base. Either way, this kind of growth can often be fun (if you forget about the actual boxes-and-packing part of moving).

❋ *Now with More Features!*

Growing doesn't always need to entail hiring staff or getting swish new digs. Sometimes your business will grow in ways that are more internal, like offering new services or products, or expanding and shifting your client base. As we discussed in Chapter 12 on customer service, your existing customers are key to the survival of your business, and selling them more or offering them more services is one of the most cost-effective and low-risk ways to expand your business—and with that, your profit margins. It is well worth doing this exercise on a regular basis with your business, no matter what your focus is.

The exercise is pretty simple: Just take a look at your existing customers and the services/products you offer, and ask yourself what more you could be doing to increase the frequency or amount of your customers' purchases. Now, we're not saying you should overcharge people; that's not going to result in sustainable growth (people can always smell a rat). A typical example of what we are talking about, and which most of us can relate to, is the hair salon. In addition to doing all that stylish cutting, coloring, and blow-drying, the salon you go to probably has some intoxicatingly scented shampoos and hair goops to keep your coif happy at home, right? Well, in addition to making it easy for you to get all your hair needs taken care of in one stop, those products also help the salon increase the average price of their sales/ interactions with you, which in turn allows them to improve their profit margins without really having to take any major leaps in staffing or floor space. That said, the salon needs to keep a balance between how much money they are likely to make off those products and how much they keep tied up in maintaining a stock of products on the shelves. Here are some other examples that should help you think about how you might expand within your current capacity.

1. For service- and consulting-based businesses, start to think about what kinds of other services you might start offering your clients. While we're all for specializing, it may be that once you've established yourself in your trade, you realize that there are services you could offer that your clients are getting elsewhere. Often clients will really appreciate being able to have you take care of a few different aspects of their work for them, and you can increase your business without having to go out and find new clients.

▶ A few years ago, we found our clients always asking us for advice about how to get their sites into Google. That was the kind of information that we were keeping on top of anyway as website designers, but we didn't really consider ourselves experts in search engine optimization. But the topic kept coming up. So we hit the books (and the web) and rounded out our skill set. Then we called up those curious clients who we knew were in the market and offered up our new services.

2. If you have a retail store, and folks keep asking you for something you don't carry, or you see a niche opening up that no one is filling, then you may want to step up to the plate.

▶ After a few years of running ads on her successful website Design Sponge, Grace Bonney noticed that she had an excellent asset up her sleeve: an enviable list of talented and popular up-and-coming designers looking to sell their wares. She decided to open up the Design Sponge Shop with the goal of selling small runs of work by the in-demand artists on her contact list. The shop is a win-win: It helps Grace in her ongoing quest to expose up-and-coming talent to the world of design lovers, it gives her readers access to the kind of work they turned to Grace to recommend, and it helped reinvigorate Grace's enthusiasm in her work—a challenge many of us have along the way.

3. For those of you making a product, this may simply mean expanding your line so that you can offer more choices to your existing customers. Whether that's offering your clothes in more sizes or more colors, or designing whole new products, if your customers are already big fans of what you're selling, chances are they'll want to check out new items too.

▶ Vancouver dreadlock experts Knotty Boy Dread Stuff had pretty much cornered the market when it came to making the best products for producing and maintaining nice-'n'-knotty tresses. And they had even reached the max when it came to dread-happy accessories like hats and beads. So: what next? Aside from just planning to find more soon-to-be-knotty heads out there, they found that they were regularly getting questions from some of their younger customers about removing their dreads for school, parents, or job interviews, and they knew there had to be a better answer than "shave it all off!" So they went into their top-secret Knotty Lab and devised a product that would actually help to undread hair: The Knotty Boy Dreadlock Removal Kit.

❋ *Cash Flow Woes*

While we started this discussion with the ever-so-optimistic prediction of extra cash lying around just waiting to be spent on financing the growth of your business, that may not always be the case. In fact, often expansion—even when it has been carefully planned and is in fact going to be totally sustainable—will place you in a temporary cash flow crunch. That may just last a month or two while your invoices catch up with your new higher capacity due to the extra staff on hand, or it may mean that you have to wait a full production cycle before you see the payoff. Either way, as long as you have solid projections that see an increase on the horizon, you don't need to get too stressed out about short-term cash flow droughts—remember, this is what credit is for, and growing your business is often very similar to starting your business in terms of having all kinds of one-time hard costs associated with it.

For those of you manufacturing a product, growth will almost always mean swimming against the cash flow current. Our close pals at Lunapads are always reminding us of how success can sometimes temporarily be quite costly. As their business continues to grow at very promising rates, they continue to need to increase their credit to reach the next level. Each time they want to increase their production run of marvelous washable pads, they have to buy more fabric, snaps, and thread than the last time. While they continue to get better and better margins on the materials they are buying as their amounts go up, they still need to lay out more and more cash each time to make their products before they can turn around and sell them. At a certain point, they realized that in order to take the next step for growth, they needed outside investment. Having tapped out their "love money" and credit card limits, they raised funds through a combination of a bank loan and an outside investor. It was in many ways a big risk for them, but one they couldn't afford not to take (what were they going to do, start saying no to women who wanted to order pads?) and one they felt very solid in taking. Depending on how much cash you need to get yourself over these humps, you very well may need to produce hard numbers for the bank (or wealthy Aunt Mabel), and either way, you should take a good hard look at your finances for your own peace of mind before you go getting all big and fancy on us.

❄ *The Never-Ending Story*

While we still don't really think "If you're not growing, you're dying" is any kind of useful credo to run your business by, we hope you'll see that growing doesn't need to look like having so many outlets of your fair-trade coffee shop on every corner that no one can go a block without being able to pop in and get one of your yummy soy lattes—though if you want to take those other guys on, we're totally behind you, baby. If you're just starting out now, and the idea of growing feels terrifyingly daunting, don't worry—you will get a sense of how your business will evolve and expand as you settle in. Being an entrepreneur by definition seems to mean that you never really rest. Just as you reach one level, you'll probably start thinking ahead to new things you can do, how you can do things better, or what else you can offer your customers. And even if it is just in little ways that don't make the front of the business pages, you'll know you are doing your best to keep your business and your customers happy.

CHAPTER 15

Celebrate Your Achievements

IF YOU'VE BEEN PAYING ATTENTION, you may have noticed that many of the chapters leading up to this one have ended with a note of congratulations. We've been trying to encourage you to acknowledge your new-entrepreneur progress in concrete ways. And we aren't doing that out of some latent, cheerleaderesque hyperenthusiasm—it's just that we've been through this ourselves, and one of the things we found most difficult was tooting our own horns. It turns out we're not alone. With all the crazy-awesome women we interviewed for this book, few of them had an answer much beyond "Well, a glass of wine is nice," when we asked them how they celebrate their remarkable achievements. We have a sneaking suspicion that this lack of high-fiving around the watercooler has something to do with gender, which makes us even more committed to the idea of helping you get your party hat on.

When you're the one in charge, you're not only in control of when, how, and whether work gets done but you're also the only one who's going to pat you on the back for a job well done, cut you a bonus check, and give you the rest of the day off. Think we're being flippant? Think again.

❀ Aw, Do I Hafta?

In your first year, when money is tight, celebrating your successes will seem like a luxury you can't afford. Later on, you may have a bit more money to go around, but no time to spare—so you'll be in much the same headspace. And once your business is established, and the pace has mellowed a bit, you could be so out of practice on the celebrating front that the whole idea will just seem bizarre and strangely self-indulgent.

See where we're going with this? There's never going to be a time when you're going to say to yourself, "Hey, I've got all this spare time and money on hand, and nothing better to spend it on than to take myself out and congratulate myself on my success as a business genius!" So you might as well start early, and get in the habit.

There are a million excuses for not celebrating, but let's go back to our mantra: You are your best employee. Now that you *are* the boss, you have to step into the role of being your own manager as well. And that means giving yourself credit for your accomplishments, from hitting your sales targets to completing a project. Try to imagine yourself as your dream boss and picture the rewards that would be showered upon star employees: Those are just the things you'll want to try to give yourself at celebration time. (Okay, so the trip to Bermuda may need to wait a bit—but maybe you can swing a visit to a spa with a sauna and steam bath, or a package of paper umbrellas to decorate homemade daiquiris for you and a couple of friends.)

Solo entrepreneurs have it tough: There's no one to tell you to go home at five o'clock, or to help you out with that uber-demanding customer. And when it comes to marking your business's milestones, you're on your own there, too.

> *Time to dream up a cheering section—a team of support-ers who will help you raise a toast to your hard work paying off. One option here is to corral a bunch of friends; another is to join (or form) a small networking group for fellow business owners. No one understands better than another entrepreneur just how much work went into your grand opening or your first hire. And if all that fails, your mom or girlfriend/boyfriend may be your best ally here.*

❀ *Ac-cent-tchu-ate the Positive*

You may not buy any of this woo-woo stuff, but we've turned into true believers when it comes to this New Age adage: What you put out into the universe will come back to you. In other words, if you want more success, project your successes out to the world. And we don't mean you should go around bragging and acting like you're bet-ter than everyone; rather, we're hoping you'll be secure enough to ac-knowledge your successes with equal measures of pride and humility.

There are two reasons we believe this works, and neither of them requires you to douse yourself in patchouli or light incense. First, the world loves a winner. When people hear that you were responsible for the flower arrangements at Mayor Chan's victory party, their es-timation of you will go up, if for no other reason than that the word "mayor" has a certain cachet. It will also let them know that you are capable of handling arrangements for large parties, and may help bring you to mind next time someone they know decides to get married or throw a big bash.

The second reason it makes sense to proclaim your successes to the world is that when you take the time to focus on your goals, you are more likely to achieve them. So if you've spent a lunch hour with a couple of colleagues celebrating your latest product launch, chances are you will return feeling upbeat and positive about the line's potential—and clearer on where you hope it will go. Every time you make the effort to talk about, write down, or otherwise communicate your dreams, you take one step toward realizing them . . . and that's not Flakey McFlakerton talking. It's simple logic: If it's on your mind, it's more likely to happen.

❀ Party Planning

We've found that the easiest way to make sure we commemorate our best moments in business is to—sigh—schedule them. And is that lame? Maybe. But when we're in business mode, there's always something work related demanding to be done, and the only way to work around that is to book a time for making merry.

For us, party time is often as simple as a nice lunch to mark the completion of a project. We'll set a date and time once the project's done, and take an hour or so out of the day to revel in the satisfaction and closure (and happy cash flow) that a finished project brings. On other occasions, we've preplanned special treats with some connection to the project: like getting makeovers done to celebrate the launch of a beauty-product website, or buying new plants for the office after wrapping up a site for a landscape designer. Whatever the specifics of the celebration in question, it goes on the to-do list alongside all our billable and administrative work, to ensure we give it equal weight.

If your work doesn't lend itself easily to the milestone framework, it can be hard to step back and recognize how far you've come. You may want to assign yourself some arbitrary celebration days, such as your company's anniversary, International Women's Day (March 8—we take the day off each year), or Friday afternoons. The main thing is to try to do something regularly, and *at least* once every three months.

It's astonishingly easy to procrastinate on this stuff. You're going to have dozens of other, "better" things to do, from balancing the books to ringing up a sale. But now that you're the one running the show, you've got to set your business's priorities, and we hope your mental health and well-being are at (or near) the top of that list. If you consistently allow your clients and customers to pull you away from looking after yourself, you're letting them set the agenda. Own your independence, and revel in your achievements; no one else is going to do it for you.

So: When's your next celebration date? And what are you going to do?

If you have employees, then you're also in charge of noting their part in helping you reach your goals—so make sure you include them in your celebrations. (That doesn't mean you can't also do something on your own.) Let them know how grateful you are for their role in your most productive month to date, or your mention in the local paper . . . and put your money where your mouth is. If you're celebrating something that boosts your revenues, consider sending a little their way, whether it takes the form of a company lunch or bonus checks. Our friends at Lunapads foot the bill for their employees to each have a nice dinner out with their honeys to acknowledge help on a big project or the completion of a really busy month.

❀ *Cynic's Corner*

If all of this seems a bit much to you, you probably need the help of an enthusiast. You know that friend you have who's always exclaiming over things and squealing in delight? That's the one. Bring that friend on board as your official sidekick, and ensure that every time you need to celebrate, your enthusiast is by your side. The more nose-to-the-grindstone you are, the more you need to observe your business milestones—otherwise it'll all pass by in a blur and you'll never enjoy your success. After all, you did get into this to enjoy yourself, didn't you? At least a little bit? (Burning out is just so much less fun.)

❀ What Are We Celebrating?

If your business doesn't operate on a project model—or even if it does—you might like to mark one of these fine occasions:

- Achieving one or more of your business goals (remember your Chapter 1 exercises?)
- Launching a new product line
- Paying off a debt
- Landing a new client
- Getting some positive press (or heck, any kind of press!)
- Meeting a financial target
- Opening a new location
- Making it through a tough week
- Firing a draining/challenging customer
- Hiring a new employee
- Taking a risk
- Launching your website
- Qualifying for a loan/line of credit
- Reaching a one- (or five-) year anniversary

Once you know what it is you're celebrating, you may want to dream up a treat that matches the occasion. Enjoying an upbeat newspaper review? Maybe renting *The Philadelphia Story* with a girlfriend and some popcorn would be a good fit. Or, if you've just fired a difficult client, soothe your nerves with a bubble bath and a glass of wine.

The key to finding just the right indulgence is to come up with something that feels special, doesn't break the bank, and, most importantly, allows you the time and space to reflect on how you got here. You don't want to just throw money around for the hell of it; the point is to glory in the feeling of satisfaction you get when you meet your goals.

❧ *Sharing the Love*

Once you've had a chance to bask in the glory of your many gifts, consider who else might benefit from hearing about your latest accomplishments. Does your new location merit a press release? (Yes indeed.) How about meeting those revenue targets? (Probably not, although if you're really raking in the profits you may want to consider pitching a profile of your company to your local business columnist.)

The media are always hungry for stories, so be on the lookout for hooks that might reel in a reporter. If you're the only place in town using organic fabrics, send out a fact sheet on the pesticides used in cotton farming, along with a press kit. Or maybe you're breaking new ground with your hiring practices; again, it might be worth contacting the press and letting them know why hiring stay-at-home moms is such a great idea.

Even if your news isn't likely to appear on television any time soon, it may still be of interest to your clientele, so think about how you can get the word out to them. Maybe you keep a mailing list (either regular post or email) that allows you to keep in touch—you did read Chapters 7 and 8, right? Try sending out a news flash about that TV celebrity who picked up an armload of your products, or the award you won for that brochure design. Your most loyal customers will be grateful for the update, and may well pass it along to other potential clients. And it will also help them feel they're part of the inner circle—the first to know when exciting new things happen—making them more likely to come back to you in the future.

❧ *Secrets of the Rah–Rah Sisterhood*

When you made your first sale, it was a big day. Ditto for the day you got your business license, and the first time you answered your phone with your company name. As time goes on, though, and work starts piling up, it's easy to start feeling blasé about new sales, fiscal solvency, and other milestones that pepper the months. One of the joys and burdens of working for yourself is that you're the company's social coordinator (on top of everything else). The trick is to think back to those first big steps, and the frisson of excitement you experienced back then. You've come a long way, and you're doing well. Make sure you're enjoying the fruits of your labor.

Come on, don't make us get our pom-poms.

CONCLUSION
What's Next?

WHERE DO YOU GO FROM HERE? Well, once you've got your business up on its feet and you've already navigated some of the challenges of keeping your business going, it's time for payback. Time for you to become one of the business experts you used to turn to.

Now, you may feel, as we once did, that the world needs another business expert like it needs another hole in the ozone layer. And that's valid, if when we say "business expert" you envision a PowerPoint monkey with a laser pointer whose vocabulary consists mainly of vapid buzzwords. But you're not one of those people. If you were, you wouldn't have made it this far through our book. We wrote this book because we feel strongly that women need more examples of the kinds of healthy business models we set out to help you build. Well, it's time for you to be one of those women showing everyone else the way.

Before we embarked on the book project, of course, we had plenty of one-on-one conversations with other business owners, as well as cocktail nights with groups of entrepreneurs. We'd been asked for advice so many times we'd lost track. We'd written articles and started a blog. We'd given workshops, attended conferences, and organized panels. All of these experiences held a common set of goals:

1. *Share, and Share Alike.* We were sharing our experiences with other business owners in the hope of learning from each other's mistakes and successes.

2. *Earn Your "Expert" Stripes.* We boosted our confidence by getting more comfortable speaking in front of people about our experiences and developing an image as experts (but not the laser pointer kind).

3. *Live the Dream.* We spread the word about our approach to business in the hope of inspiring others and finding like-minded colleagues.

Once your business is firmly established, you should be ready to engage in some similar activities to connect you with your peers in a nonmarketing capacity—if you haven't already. Let's look at some of the options available to you.

If you're totally uninterested in sharing your experiences with others, that's fine—we're not here to guilt-trip you into being someone you're not. However, do keep in mind that there is value in getting out there and getting some outside stimulus, because at a certain point, you and your business can start to stagnate. If you find you're running low on the kind of energy that sparked your initial foray into business ownership, consider making some connections with other entrepreneurial types and giving yourself the opportunity to refuel.

❧ One-on-One Mentoring

When we hear the word "mentoring," the image that springs most quickly to mind is of an older, wiser person coaching a younger one. This can be a great approach if you can find the right partner. Often these types of connections are facilitated through larger business associations, particularly those that serve new entrepreneurs, so if you're interested in "adopting" a newbie, try phoning around to see who offers mentorship programs in your area.

We're not going to dwell too long on this type of mentoring, though, because it's rare to find an entrepreneur in the first few years of business who has the time and energy to take it on. We're guessing that at this point, you're looking for something with a little less commitment.

BUT I'M NOT AN EXPERT!

You may not feel prepared to get up and talk about your business as though you've met every challenge there is to meet. So what? There's nothing fun about a know-it-all, anyway. (And people who call themselves experts deserve to be met with skepticism.) We've always felt that you learn the most from those who know just how much they don't know. You've got to start somewhere, and chances are, if you've made it this far, you know a lot.

There's a lot to be said for telling your story honestly and humbly. Sharing your mistakes and your low points will mean a great deal to those who are starting out and scared stiff of failing; they'll see there's light at the end of the tunnel and that there's such a thing as life after mess-ups. Your success stories, and tips on what worked, will help them get started in the right direction and avoid potential pitfalls.

You don't have to believe you're an expert to start helping less experienced entrepreneurs—you just have to believe you've done at least a couple of things right, and at least one thing wrong, and be willing to tell your story.

When your friends and acquaintances ask you for advice, make a mental note of the questions they put forward. Are there recurring themes? You may just be an expert and not know it yet. If everyone's turning to you for the answers, chances are you know something worth sharing with the world.

Just do us a favor, okay?

Skip the PowerPoint.

❀ *Volunteer Positions*

Although this isn't, strictly speaking, a "mentoring" outlet, there are lots of business associations and nonprofit groups on the lookout for bright, business-minded volunteers. These can be a great way to meet colleagues and share ideas while contributing to a good cause.

Both of us have spent a good chunk of our less-than–plentiful spare time volunteering on boards and committees for nonprofit groups, and apart from the rewards of helping them do good deeds, we discovered there were also personal and business-related benefits to lending a hand.

First, volunteering for nonprofits is a great way to hone your collaboration skills. As a business owner, it's easy to get used to having your own way a lot of the time, and it can be good to stay in practice when it comes to teamwork. You may also come in contact with people you wouldn't normally meet during the course of your workday, and that serves the dual purposes of providing you with new contacts—who might someday bring you an unexpected business lead—and shifting your usual frame of reference, which can really get the creative juices flowing.

You may also develop other skills you didn't know you had. Nonprofits tend to rely on their supporters to wear many hats, so you may be called on to help with, say, event planning and drumming up sponsorships—which will do wonders for your ability to organize that workshop series you've been thinking about.

But the other, subtler thing you gain from this type of work is an increased sense of comfort around being an expert in your field. Because you're likely to be the only representative of your business niche, others in the group will look to you for special insights. (After all, you're sure to know more than they do about sourcing shampoo bottles, using various printing techniques, or whatever it is you do best.) When you're an entrepreneur, you're forced to do a lot of flying by the seat of your pants, so the benefits of *somebody* thinking you know what you're doing cannot be underestimated. We all need a little moral support to get us through the day.

Finally, it can be strategic for your business to partner up with a charity that works in a related field—or that could use your products or services. Julia Beardwood told us that she sought out a company that was making "green" products because she thought their packaging could use some help, and she was excited about the idea of doing some environmentally focused work and adding that to her portfolio.

Finding the right charitable partner is a win–win situation, because it can challenge you to develop new skills and meet new people at the same time that it enables you to give something back to your community. And who knows? You may also get the opportunity to raise the profile of your business among like-minded people.

> *In the early days of our business, Emira pitched in to help a local society supporting women in technology. The group hosted monthly meetings featuring speakers and networking opportunities for women in high-tech careers. Her contributions meant that our interests as entrepreneurs and web designers were represented in the choice of speakers and event themes, and ensured that the group remained relevant for other business owners and gals in web-related fields.*

❧ *The Writer Within*

Another way to share your wisdom is through the written word. From your local paper to online e-zines, there's a wealth of outlets on the lookout for fresh perspectives on business—and plenty of budding entrepreneurs thirsty for stories, both cautionary and inspiring. If you're an introverted type, or just fond of writing down your thoughts, this could be a fit for you.

Beyond the direct benefit to your readers, there are also some perks to moonlighting as a business writer, and the biggest one is that you'll become known as an expert. (There's that word again, dagnabit.) Having your name on the byline of an article can give you an "official" air that marks you as worthy of representing your field. This can help attract customers as well as potential suppliers, staff, and partners. It can also help promote your brand in a less direct sense—so if you own an accessories store and can wrangle yourself a fashion advice column, your readers will come to appreciate your style better, which will in turn help them to spread the word about you to like-minded friends.

Two caveats here: One, think about how much time you can afford to spend writing, as it can be a consuming effort. A weekly column will take several hours a week to write. A regular gig may be more than you can handle, so you may want to start with a few freelance contributions and see how it feels.

Two: Don't expect to be paid well (or even at all) for your contributions, at least at first. If you write a regular column that starts to draw a crowd, you'll be in a position to lobby for higher pay—but many e-zines and smaller-distribution publications are short on cash and rely on volunteer submissions. If compensation is on your mind, be sure to check out the possibilities beforehand.

❀ Workshops and Conferences and Panels, Oh My!

No matter what your specialty is, chances are there are others out there who want to learn about it—and how you got into it. Whether you run a flower shop or manage a roster of up-and-coming bands, there are plenty of topics on which people would love to hear you wax poetic. Keep your ear to the ground and watch for workshops and conferences where you might hold forth on your favorite subject. (If you're out of the loop on these kinds of events, check in with your local business association or chamber of commerce, or just snoop around online for a while.)

WHERE DO I START?

If you're still not sure what approach is the best fit for you, try this: Meditate for a moment on the questions you're asked most often about your work. Do people want to know how you got financing for your eco-landscaping business? Or are they more interested in how you select plants that don't need too much watering? Spend some time mulling over the stuff that seems to interest people most, and then figure out how to convey that information to the people who want it. Maybe it makes the most sense to lead a workshop at a gardening center—or perhaps you'd be better off giving a talk at a business conference or writing an article.

If the idea of leading a one-hour workshop feels like scaling Mount Everest, try breaking it down into chunks: Come up with four or five topics you can talk about for ten minutes apiece, and leave some time for questions. You'd be surprised how quickly an hour goes when you're talking about yourself—er, your business.

Be prepared to tailor your topic to your audience—the event's organizers should be able to help you here. If you're addressing a broad-based group, you'll need to focus on generalities everyone can relate to, whereas if you're speaking to your peers, you can probably afford to get specific.

❋ *Welcome Aboard*

We're so glad you're here. Honestly. When we first sat down to write this book we were fueled by the idea of sharing the stories of the incredibly smart, successful businesswomen we knew. As we got further into things and had the chance to speak to an even wider circle of talented business gals, our excitement only grew. There truly are so freakin' many of us out there starting and running businesses that buck the mainstream business models—and we couldn't be more thrilled about it. It is our deepest hope that this book helps those numbers soar. We are tickled, more than you know, that you picked this book up to help you run your business your way, and now we want you to carry this mission forward and spread the word among your business-curious friends. Last time we checked, women running small, successful businesses that allow them to take control of their own lives still aren't making it onto the front pages of the business section of the newspaper. That doesn't mean we're not out there, and it certainly doesn't mean we can't learn from one another in a quest to grow even stronger.

So the next time you meet a woman who is running her own business, congratulate her on her success. And if she tries to play it down and tell you, "Well, it's really not a big deal, I just work for myself/run a small store/make this line of products that only a niche market knows about," push her modesty aside and tell her you think she's awesome. And feel free to mention that you know at least another two businesswomen who think so too.

Resource Guide

Over the years we've been in business for ourselves, we've read countless books, websites, and magazines that purported to impart business wisdom and inspiration—some of them were awesome, while others wasted our time. We'd love to save you the trouble of separating the wheat from the chaff, so we've compiled a list of our favorite resources. Many of them delve more deeply into areas that we could only touch on in the preceding pages: topics like personal finance and the exciting world of business insurance.

The other resource we'd very much like to point you to is our website: www.laurenandemira.com. We've been writing a business blog there since 2006. It is an ever-growing archive of our thoughts, advice, and favorite links, along with comments and ideas shared by our fabulous readers. The site also contains worksheets, sample budgets, and various resources that just wouldn't fit into the pages of our beloved book. And because the web evolves constantly—unlike books, which need to be marked "final edit" and sent off to the printer—we'll be adding to the list you see here over time as we come across new resources and books worth sharing.

❀ *Writing a Business Plan*

It's not for everyone, but many entrepreneurs find that writing a formal business plan is the quickest path from dreaming to doing. It's also a must if you're seeking start-up funding. Here's the best business plan resource we've come across. . . .

Interactive Business Planner

www.canadabusiness.ca/ibp/

> Even the U.S. Small Business Administration (www.sba. gov)—a great resource unto itself—recommends the Government of Canada's Interactive Business Planner, which we used when we first started Raised Eyebrow. This free tool guides you through the process of writing a business plan step by step, and allows you to save your work and log back in to view it anytime, online.

❀ *Government Resources*

Whether you're looking to familiarize yourself with tax forms or looking for government-funded programs for new businesses, plenty of the most valuable stuff around can be found on these government-run websites. Be prepared, though: Nothing can really make this stuff any less dry.

U.S.A.

SCORE: Counselors to America's Small Business

www.score.org

> This nonprofit organization provides tons of free resources, as well as counseling services for small business owners and self-employed people. Highly recommended.

IRS: Small Business and Self-Employed One-Stop Resource

www.irs.gov/businesses/small/

Everything you need to know to keep your taxes in order. Don't miss the "Online Classroom," a step-by-step lesson in what every small business owner needs to know about all things tax related. And believe it or not, it's actually very accessible.

Women's Business Enterprise National Council

www.wbenc.org

The WBENC offers certification for women-owned businesses, which can help land you government contracts (if that's your sort of thing).

U.S. Small Business Administration

www.sba.gov

If you're in the market for training, loans, and/or government contracts, this is the place to start.

Business.gov

www.business.gov

A site run by the U.S. Small Business Administration, but that's easier to navigate, and chock-full of helpful tools and info on everything from licenses and permits—the site has an easy-to-use tool to help you find the right info for your business, based on location and business type—to small business grants, workplace health and safety, and much more.

CANADA

Women's Enterprise Centre (B.C.)

www.womensenterprise.ca

Several Canadian provinces have Women's Enterprise Centres—we just happen to live in B.C., so we can speak personally to the value of the services this group provides. From online resources to workshops to phone counseling from seasoned entrepreneurs, the WEC is an invaluable resource for Canadian women in business.

❀ Legal Advice

Nolo Press

www.nolo.com

> Nolo writes about the law in accessible language, and offers a great deal of very helpful legal advice free on its website. From patents and trademarks to ownership structures and your legal duties as an employer, they've got you covered. They sell legal guides as well, should you need more in-depth information.

❀ Licenses and Registration

The processes for obtaining the right licenses and permits vary widely from state to state, so we simply can't list them all here—but SCORE (www.score.org) has a helpful and thorough list of all the hoops you'll need to jump through. Just head to their home page and search for "permit." Your next-best bet is to run a web search on your city's name and the phrase "business license," e.g., "Minneapolis business license"—that should pull up the relevant government website that will get you started in the right direction.

❀ Copyrights, Trademarks, and Patents

Cover your butt—make sure your precious goodies (a.k.a. your bread and butter) are protected by law. You'll sleep so much better at night.

WORLDWIDE

Creative Commons

www.creativecommons.org

> Established in 2002, Creative Commons allows content creators (i.e., writers, artists, photographers, designers, filmmakers, musicians, etc.) to label their work on a spectrum of rights, from "all rights reserved" to "some rights reserved"

to "no rights reserved." Their website puts it best: "With a Creative Commons license, you keep your copyright but allow people to copy and distribute your work provided they give you credit—and only on the conditions you specify."

U.S.A.

U.S. Copyright Office

www.copyright.gov

If it's intellectual property you want to protect, this is the place to start. Essential reading for writers, composers, and artists, in particular.

United States Patent and Trademark Office

www.uspto.gov

Your first stop for all things trademark and patent related. You can even file your trademarks online.

CANADA

Canadian Intellectual Property Office

www.cipo.gc.ca

CIPO manages the vast majority of intellectual property rights in Canada, including copyright, patents, and trademarks, as well as industrial designs.

❀ *Personal Finance*

We assume this is pretty obvious by now, but if you're going to be the boss of you, you also need to be the boss of your bank account. Big time. While you ought to set your business finances up to run separately from your personal finances, getting your personal finances and financial goals in order before you take the big plunge is a must. We don't mean you need to have a year's salary socked away or anything, but it's oh so important to have a firm grasp on what kind of cash you need to bring in to pay off your debts and save something for a rainy day, and eventually what you'll need to take care of your future retired self.

One of the myths about reading personal finance books is that you need to have an abundance of personal finance to bother with them. Well, consider that myth busted now. Whether you start by taking control of your daunting debt or your extra savings, know that taking positive action with your finances is definitely not just for the rich.

On My Own Two Feet: A Modern Girl's Guide to Personal Finance by Manisha Thakor and Sharon Kedar (Adams Business)

There are lots of excellent resources out there to help guide you through the world of personal finance. What's great about Manisha and Sharon's book—aside from it being authored specifically for women—is that it's short, to the point, and has lots of action items to help you grasp the theory and apply it to your wallet. Also, they don't assume you're an idiot, or rolling in cash just looking for a place to invest. We like that.

She Laughed All the Way to the Bank: Financial Empowerment for Canadian Women by Cindy Skrukwa (Raincoast)

Written for a Canadian audience (hello, fellow Canucks!), this now-oldie-but-goody is sadly out of print, but you can still find copies of it on ye olde Internet. Like *On My Own Two Feet, She Laughed* is aimed at helping empower women—regardless of their current financial state—to take control of their finances. It will help you see the steps between here and your dreams, and give you the tools to make some of them a reality.

Smart Women Finish Rich: 9 Steps to Achieving Financial Security and Funding Your Dreams by David Bach (Doubleday)

Cheesy cover alert! Okay, while this series (there's also a *Smart Couples Finish Rich* and *Start Late, Finish Rich,* etc.) is a bit too gimmicky for our usual tastes, Lauren swears by some of the basics of organizing your finances she got out of this book—in particular, the filing system for financial records.

The author also makes a point of insisting that you get clear on your personal values before setting your financial goals. So, while it may not be an obvious choice, it's well worth a look. (And if you're like us, i.e., guilty of judging books by their covers, do what we did: Take it out of the library.)

BANK WEBSITES

While they're not necessarily the sexiest of websites, bank websites contain a host of financial tools for the eager beavers among you. With everything from retirement-planning calculators to loan and mortgage calculators (and sometimes rent vs. owning comparisons), banks have lots of fancy tools that you can plug dreamland numbers into and see what comes out the other side. Great for helping you see just how that extra $20 a week in savings or on debt payments can pay off in the long run.

❋ *Health Insurance*

Ah, the great dividing line between Canada and the United States—no, not the 49th parallel, universal healthcare. We confess to being woefully ignorant of Stateside healthcare options, so we turned to our friend and colleague Michelle Goodman, author of *The Anti 9-to-5 Guide* (see below) for advice. She kindly pointed us to these resources for getting health coverage when you're self-employed:

Access to Health Insurance/Resources for Care
www.ahirc.org

A huge database of affordable health insurance options, organized by state. Not only does it include information for small businesses and self-employed individuals, but there's also a ton of info for other underserved groups, from people with HIV, to immigrants and refugees, to people with substance abuse problems—so it's worth spreading the word about this excellent resource.

PROFESSIONAL ORGANIZATIONS

Depending on your industry, you may be able to access affordable health insurance by joining a professional association. There are associations for people in almost every field, from graphic designers to farm workers, so if you're not already aware of associations in your area, you can try a web search and see what comes up. For example, free-lance writers and editors can get insurance through Media Bistro (national: www.mediabistro.com) or the Freelancers Union (New York: www.freelancersunion.org).

❋ *General Business Resources*

The Anti 9-to-5 Guide: Practical Career Advice for Women Who Think Outside the Cube by Michelle Goodman (Seal Press)

> Just when we were going on at length about the lack of smart, fun, and useful info for the would-be self-employed gal, out came Michelle's *Anti 9-to-5 Guide.* If you're thinking freelancing is more your gig than small business, then Michelle's book is for you. Full disclosure: We've had the pleasure of getting to know Michelle personally since her book came out, and as cocheerleaders in the world of self-employed women, we became fast friends. But don't for one minute think that the bias of friendship would lead us to include this book out of hand. Michelle's book is so full of useful information about everything from finding the career that might work for you to getting your taxes in order that we found several pages worth tagging with Post-it notes.

Small Time Operator: How to Start Your Own Business, Keep Your Books, Pay Your Taxes and Stay Out of Trouble! by Bernard B. Kamoroff (Bell Springs Publishing)

> This book was recommended to us by Jenny Hart, of Sublime Stitching, as an invaluable resource for answering common business questions like "How do I pay my taxes as a business owner?" "Should I incorporate?" "Do I need a permit to do

this?" etc. If a recommendation from the highly successful and oh-so-smart Jenny Hart isn't enough for you, Amazon tells us this book is now in its twenty-seventh edition. Seriously. Kamoroff will not give you examples of guerrilla marketing on the cheap, nor is his target women business owners specifically, but when it comes to the nuts and bolts of business hoop-jumping, he's got it covered.

Business for Beginners: From Research and Business Plans to Money, Marketing and the Law (US Edition) and **Business for Beginners: A Simple Step-by-Step Guide to Starting a Small Business** (Canadian Edition) by Frances McGuckin

Though not specifically aimed at the female business owner, *Business for Beginners* is a volume that was helpful for us in the early days; it combines many of the basics around taxes, insurance, finances, incorporation, etc., all in one place—and the two editions provide concrete information for American and Canadian business. You're not going to find sassy advice here, but you will find plenty of answers to common bureaucracy-related questions.

Small Giants: Companies That Choose to Be Great Instead of Big by Bo Burlingham (Portfolio Trade)

Among the shelves of books touting growth, growth, growth, this book stands out as an inspiration for every entrepreneur who believes there's value in keeping a lid on corporate sprawl. Bo Burlingham profiles some incredible businesses—from Ani DiFranco's Righteous Babe Records to Zingerman's Deli and Clif Bar—that made a conscious decision to stay small and remain true to their values, despite pressure to get bigger. It's also engagingly written by a veteran business journalist who does a beautiful job of conveying the personalities behind each business.

Inc. magazine

www.inc.com

> To be perfectly honest, we don't read much in the way of business magazines (they tend to be a little too heavy on the suits and mergers for our tastes), but we love the website for *Inc.* magazine—it's full of incredibly helpful articles and how-to guides for entrepreneurs, and it's impressively easy to get around, given the depth and breadth of information. We also love their email newsletters.

ReCourses

www.recourses.com

> If your business falls in the category of creative consultancy, as ours does, we can't recommend this firm's website highly enough. Their white papers offer some of the most valuable business advice we've encountered anywhere.

❀ *Business Resources for Crafters*

Craft Inc.: Turn Your Creative Hobby into a Business by Meg Mateo Ilasco (Chronicle Books)

> An indispensable handbook for craft entrepreneurs, *Craft Inc.* provides detailed and specific guidelines for starting a successful craft business—from keeping your creative vision alive to navigating tradeshows and sourcing supplies.

Craft Mafia

www.craftmafia.com

> The first Craft Mafia started in 2003 in Austin, Texas, with nine crafty, entrepreneurial women joining forces to support each other's work; now there are at least forty Craft Mafia groups across the United States, Canada, and the U.K. Check the site to see if there's one near you.

Craftster

www.craftster.org

A long-running online forum for craft/DIY projects—here you'll find tons of project ideas and how-to guides, and most importantly, a community of passionate, committed crafters. Don't miss the "Crafty Business Advice" forum.

Etsy

www.etsy.com

An online marketplace for all things handmade, Etsy was designed to help crafters connect with buyers. Creating an online store couldn't be simpler, and the fees are low enough that even hobbyists and part-time crafters can afford to get in on the action. They've also got great forums—and other resources—for crafty businesspeople. (For more on using Etsy to sell your goodies, flip ahead to the "e-commerce on the cheap" section.)

The Sampler

www.homeofthesampler.com

Get the word out about your business by contributing samples of your goods (or promotional materials) and pooling them with other DIY goodies. The sample packs are sent out to subscribers, contributors, and members of the press.

Glitter

www.supernaturale.com/glitter/

Another fantastic craft-related forum, Glitter has a section called "The Business Side" that's a must-read for crafty businesswomen.

❀ *Resources for Moms*

While we expect moms to make use of the other resources round here too, let's face it: Moms have some extra balls in the air when it comes to being their own bosses. Many of the entrepreneurial moms we spoke to found that networking with others in similar situations has been vital. If you aren't in a place where meeting other mom-bosses is easy to do in the flesh, check out these websites:

Mothering
www.mothering.com

> A site for all issues related to mothering and becoming a mom; the real gem here for the working mom is the forums. There they have spaces for moms to set up local discussions for different cities/areas; if there isn't one there for your location already, try starting one up. Often the moms will get together in real life for playdates and group activities, which might help you meet other moms in your situation with whom you can share resources—like swapping childcare hours for alone-work-time hours—and empathize about the unique challenges of squeezing business calls into nap times. The community is very active about supporting WAHM (work-at-home moms), so you're likely to find some kin here. Do take note, however, that mothering.com is a site geared more at alternative lifestyles and parenting, so if the idea of vegetarian babies and shared family beds gives you the wiggins, move on.

Workitmom.com
www.workitmom.com

> Unlike Mothering, which is a broader parenting resource, this site is all about working and moms. (The site address probably gave that away already, huh?) Full of resources, articles, and again, discussion forums, the site isn't exclusively for entrepreneurial moms, but there are lots of them on there. If you are an entrepreneurial mom, this may also be a great place to get some PR about your business, so include them on your list for press releases, email announcements, etc.

❈ *Marketing*

There are mountains of books about marketing and branding out there, and most of them feel to us a bit like they were written by your stereotypical, much-maligned used car salesman. Few of them speak about marketing from your heart, feeling proud of your products/services, or using nonstandard/el cheapo ways to get the word out. In fact, that's why we have an entire section on marketing in this here book. To that end, one of the resource tips we'd like to give you around marketing is to use whatever creative processes work for you. If you're having trouble figuring out what colors should be on your business card, go to the library and search the design, interior decorating, art, or travel section—or whatever section appeals to you. Take out a bunch of books with lots of pictures and see what colors/moods and looks feel right to you. If you're stuck on what an ad should look like, flip through magazines to see what others are doing, invest in a few of those pricey graphic design magazines, and check out some of the best designs in the field. Our point: Marketing is a creative pursuit. Don't feel limited by how-to books on selling widgets; get your creative juices flowing and see what happens.

Make a Name for Yourself: Eight Steps Every Woman Needs to Create a Personal Brand Strategy for Success by Robin Fisher Roffer (Broadway)

> Off the bat, let us just say that we are typically *very* skeptical about any book that promises its knowledge comes in the form of a numbered list. Because of that, we likely never would have picked up *Make a Name for Yourself* if it hadn't been recommended by a trusted colleague. The book is not a traditional marketing book, and in fact is not aimed specifically at entrepreneurs, but rather at women interested in success in their careers regardless of who writes their paycheck. That said, for those of us who see our own personalities and vision closely wrapped up in the identity of our business/services/products, there are some useful exercises in the book.

Marketing Genius by Peter Fisk (Capstone)

If you're looking to really immerse yourself in the world of marketing, this book does a good job of talking about marketing principles without focusing exclusively on examples that only big businesses can learn from. One of the things that set this book apart from many of the others filling the marketing shelves is that Fisk actually spends some time discussing the ethics of marketing.

Duct Tape Marketing Blog

www.ducttapemarketing.com/blog

John Jantsch is the author of the book *Duct Tape Marketing: The World's Most Practical Small Business Marketing Guide,* but frankly, we think his blog is a better resource. He's a marketing guy, he speaks in marketing speak, and he's a bit of a rock star in the web world, but he's got some goods to back up the fame. It's well worth spending some regular time weekly or monthly thinking about how you market your business, and checking in on John's blog is a good way to get your thoughts going.

Guy Kawasaki's Blog

blog.guykawasaki.com

If John Jantsch is a bit of a web rock star, Guy Kawasaki is Elvis and the Beatles put together. Guy stays on top of web technologies and marketing in particular. So if you're wondering how you might work Facebook into your marketing plan, Guy will have ideas. He's also got brilliant advice on public speaking, should that factor into your marketing (or perhaps PR) plans.

Media Bistro

www.mediabistro.com/bbs/

This site is aimed at people working in the media, especially freelancers—but anyone can glean excellent advice from the forum. Of particular interest is the "Publicists' Corner" section, where you can get expert tips on how to get mentioned in magazines and newspapers.

❋ *How to Set Up Your Own Blog*

If you don't already have a blog and are thinking it might be a good part of your marketing plan, then you've got many options before you. And fortunately, the price tags start at "FREE." Each of these blogging tools has its advantages and disadvantages, and they all offer free trials, so it's worth getting a free account and playing around before you make a final decision about which tool is best for you.

Here's a list of the more common and reliable blogging tools at press time:

Blogger
www.blogger.com

> One of the originals. Absolutely free, and quick and easy to get up and running.

Movable Type
www.movabletype.org

> This one requires having the software set up on a hosting account somewhere. The hosting will cost you monthly; currently, the software is free. If you're not super tech-savvy and don't have a pal who can help you out with installing and configuring software, you may want to move along to Movable Type's cousin, TypePad.

TypePad
www.typepad.com

> TypePad is essentially a hosted version of Movable Type. That means they've already taken care of setting it up for you somewhere, and your subscription fees cover the cost of the hosting. Costs range from $4.95 per month to $29.95 per month for varying levels of service. You can start out with a free trial.

WordPress
www.wordpress.org

> At WordPress, you can either download their free blogging software and set it up on a hosting account somewhere—as

with Movable Type you'll need to pay the hosting fees and learn to install the software—or you can hie thee to www.wordpress.com and get a hosted WordPress blog, which like TypePad is preinstalled for you for free.

❋ *E-commerce on the Cheap*

We often tell our clients that e-commerce, done well, is really expensive. And if you need to set up e-commerce at a totally professional level, that is true. Fortunately for you, there are lots of ways to dip your toes into e-commerce for much lower costs, to see what the web may hold for you in the ways of revenue, before you make a serious investment. There are two main pieces to e-commerce: the online account that allows you to take money (important!) and the actual site and shopping cart that allow you to display your wares and sell them to your lovely customers.

HELPING YOU (LEGALLY) TAKE OTHER PEOPLE'S MONEY ONLINE

Having a Visa terminal for your store doesn't mean you can accept credit cards online. Banks consider "merchant terminals" (the kind that live on the counter in your shop) and "online accounts" (the kind that let folks securely enter their credit card number on a website) to be totally different things. If you have the former, you still need to the get the latter in order to process payments online. And banks—or the financial institution you use—will charge you additional fees for that separate account. Kinda lame, *non?* We totally encourage you to speak to your bank about getting online merchant accounts if you think that's what you need, but we'll warn you that you should figure out the fees and decide how much volume in business you'll need to do to make the additional fees worthwhile.

If getting more accounts (and paying more fees) with the bank isn't going to work for you, fear not! There's always PayPal. Seriously. If it works for eBay, it can work for you. The thing that's nice about

PayPal is that they only charge you a percentage of your sales; they don't charge you for keeping the account active even when you have no sales. And while they do get to take a portion of your money just for transferring money from your customers to you, you can recoup some of that cost in how you price your goods.

As of the writing of this book Google had also set up a similar payment system called Google Checkout, but we've not had the chance to check that out, as it isn't available for us folks north of the border.

ONLINE SHOPPING CARTS/E-COMMERCE SYSTEMS

If you've got a pal who is a whiz at these things, or if your primary source of business is going to be online and you have the funds to invest in building a kick-ass custom e-commerce store, go for it! After all, this is what we do for a living—we're big fans of the Net. That said, if you're not sure how things are going to go, and you don't want to make a big investment up front, there are a couple of great (cheap!) services out there for the trying. Both allow you to set up free accounts and play around a bit before you commit. One of the other big advantages of these systems—aside from their low cost of entry—is that they help expose your goods to the public, as there are many folks who browse these sites for the perfect hot pink enamel lightning bolt earrings, framed lithographs, or banjo strap.

Etsy
www.etsy.com

> Tell me you've heard of Etsy by now? Etsy, the place where you can sell anything handmade in your own little Etsy store. As with PayPal, there's no cost to get started; they simply take a portion of your sales. Again, you should work that fee into your cost of goods sold.

Shopify.com
www.shopify.com

> Shopify is quite similar to Etsy in how they make their money, i.e., they take a percentage of all your sales. It's

different from Etsy in that you can choose from a number of templates to change the look and feel of the site to suit your liking—and a Shopify site will let you have a few extra basic pages for things like a bio page, information about your products, shipping policies, and so on. In fact, you can even run a blog through your Shopify site. Shopify does not include the same stipulations about selling only handmade goods. You can also—unlike with Etsy—give your site its own personalized site address: you know, a nice www.myfancywebsite.com kind of thing.

❃ *Networking and Swapping Services*

Sometimes what you need most is a little help from your friends. If you need some help finding the right people to talk to, start here.

The Switchboards
www.theswitchboards.com
> The Switchboards is an online community for women entrepreneurs, where you can seek out people who are willing to share their expertise—and possibly even swap products and services with you. Who says you can't trade legal advice in exchange for a one-of-a-kind wristwatch?

Upcoming
www.upcoming.yahoo.com
> Find out about entrepreneurial and networking events in your area, and add them to your calendar. Of course, you can also promote your own events, should you decide to start your own haven for like-minded entrepreneurs.

Meetup
www.meetup.com
> Networking give you the heebie-jeebies? Start by finding people with similar interests; visit Meetup and locate groups in your area that cater to your particular persuasions. Great

for hobbies, too, but try searching for "entrepreneurs" and see what comes up. (Of course, if you don't see anything interesting, start your own Meetup group!)

❀ *Hiring and Retaining Employees*

Love 'Em or Lose 'Em: Getting Good People to Stay by Beverly Kaye and Sharon Jordan-Evans (Berrett Koehler)

The hard truth of most HR books is that they're painfully cheesy and almost exclusively geared toward managing employees or acquiring leadership skills for large corporate settings. And frankly, a lot of the advice on managing office politics and team-building exercises just is not going to apply to your small company. That said, although *Love 'Em or Lose 'Em* assumes you're in a bigger company, a lot of the advice can be extrapolated for those of us with one or two people on staff. With concrete advice for hiring, firing, and interviewing employees, and tools and tips for making sure you're appreciating your staff, there's some good stuff here. One warning: Their diversity chapter feels a bit antiquated, but maybe we feel that way 'cause we figure you're ahead of the curve on issues of discrimination and diversity in the workplace.

Hiring at Monster.com
http://hiring.monster.com

Monster.com's "Monster for Employers" site is mostly aimed at getting you to post jobs on their site, but they also have a great little resource center (yep, just click on the "Resource Center" link) with some wickedly useful articles on recruiting and retaining the best employees possible.

❀ *Our Glorious Colleagues*

Hopefully, by the time you've arrived here, you'll already know just how brilliant the women are who agreed to be profiled in this book. Their wisdom and generosity humbled us beyond belief and kept us committed to this project when we had grown tired of listening to ourselves talk. If you'd like to learn more about them or their businesses, or want to send some love their way in the form of supporting their fabulous ventures, here's where to find them all:

Julia Beardwood, Beardwood & Co., LLC
www.beardwood.com

Alex Beauchamp, mistress of many a web empire
www.hyggehouse.com
www.girlsguidetocitylife.com
www.alexthegirl.com
www.anothergirlatplay.com

Grace Bonney, Design Sponge
www.designspongeonline.com

Elizabeth Clark, Bring Your Own Bag
www.bringyourownbag.ca

Cinnamon Cooper, Poise
www.poise.cc

Teri Dimalanta, Giddy Giddy and Kukunest
www.giddygiddy.com
www.kukunest.com

Aimee Dolby, Betsy Ross Patterns
www.betsyrosspatterns.com

Jenny Hart, Sublime Stitching
www.sublimestitching.com

Adrianna Hepper, Knotty Boy Dread Stuff
www.knottyboy.com

Hannah Howard, Lizzie Sweet
www.lizziesweet.com

Jennifer LaBelle, Romp
www.rompbklyn.com

Valérie Parizeault, Rose Flash
www.roseflash.ca

Megan Reardon, The Organized Knitter
www.organizedknitter.com

Madeleine Shaw and Suzanne Siemens, Lunapads International Products Ltd.
www.lunapads.com

Beverley Steinhoff, Broadway @ Yew Chiropractic & Massage
www.vancouverbackpain.com

Trish Tacoma, Smoking Lily
www.smokinglily.com

Tiffany Threadgould, RePlayGround
www.replayground.com

Signy Wilson
www.signywilson.com

Acknowledgments

❋ *Resounding choruses of thanks to:*

Our mentors and teachers in business: Madeleine Shaw and Suzanne Siemens at Lunapads, Frances Horner and Maryse Cardin at Turtle & Hare Creative, Cathy Grant, Nancy Bradshaw, Signy Wilson, Trent Berry, Beverley Steinhoff, and the original Honeypot crew. We're honored to call all of you friends as well as teachers. Thank you for the endless supply of brilliant advice and even better company.

All the women we interviewed and whose contributions ended up in these pages; our appreciation for your openness, honesty, generosity, and wisdom simply cannot be overstated. The process of doing interviews for this book was an incredibly affirming one. It's one thing to suspect that there are legions of smart, savvy businesswomen out there; it's quite another to have the privilege of speaking with them personally. (To learn more about these extraordinary women, please turn to the end of the Resource Guide.)

Seal Press, who took a chance on a pair of newcomers and made us feel like part of the team. We are honored and delighted to be Seal Press authors. Special thanks to Brooke Warner and Anne Connolly, for their thoughtful and careful shepherding and unflagging enthusiasm. Thanks, too, to our steadfast and sharp-shooting agent, Robert

Mackwood, who helped us keep the faith and think bigger than we'd previously thought possible.

The professionals who have helped make our business so much stronger, saved us many sleepless nights, and taught us a great deal in the process: Maike Engelbrecht and the crew at Best Books, Inc.—you have done so much more for us than you know. Janice Miller, our beloved and trusted accountant. Gary Dunn, our lovely, clever, and always-cheerful lawyer. Signy Wilson (again), our business coach, without whom we would not dream or dare as much. Dr. Beverley, who single-handedly saved our careers several times over with her chiropractic kung fu.

Our South by Southwest copanelists: Alex Beauchamp, Jenny Hart, and Vickie Howell. We're so lucky to have crossed paths with your fabulous selves. Alex: We owe you a pony.

Our clients and colleagues, who make our work life a joy. Our staff, Chris, Ariane, Colin, and Melanie without whom we would quite simply not have been capable of finding the time to write—and who have brought our business to another level. Ariane Khachatourians, for her tireless help transcribing interviews. We promise they're all done now.

Our writer friends, who generously shared wisdom and advice, and commiserated when we thought we would never find our way to the end: Heather Corinna, T. L. Cowan, Amanda Gibbs, Michelle Goodman, Abigail Kinch, Inga Muscio, Cheryl Rossi, Annemarie Tempelman-Kluit, and Gayla Trail.

❀ Emira thanks:

I'll never forget the spark that passed between Lauren and me in the moment we decided to strike out on our own, together. As soon as the words "Why don't we try doing this our way?" were uttered, we knew there was no going back. What I didn't fully know at that time was what a truly excellent choice I had made in finding a business partner, coauthor, and friend like her to share this ride with. I am a lucky girl.

As I voraciously devoured Marxist feminist theory and cultural studies in university, I never, ever thought I would become a businessperson—let alone write a business book—but I have been so very lucky to have the people in my life who helped show me that business didn't need to be about faceless corporations and money alone. These folks modeled the possibilities that helped guide me to where I am today. There are many stars in that galaxy, but the brightest ones are decidedly Madeleine and Suzanne at Lunapads. Not only have they been there to dole out hands-on advice and encouragement, they also had the faith to hire us to work for them. For both ends of our relationship I am truly grateful. I also have to give particular thanks to my elders: my grandpa Jack—a businessman to be reckoned with—whose constant refrain of "Raise your rates" eventually did sink in, and my grandma, Martha, a woman who may not have run a business per se, but whose wisdom, work ethic, and common sense cannot be overvalued, and have helped me put things in much-needed perspective more than once.

There are also the many friends and loved ones in my life who have helped support me along the path from fledgling entrepreneur to established businessperson, and from wannabe writer to published author (!). My mom, who showed me the value of financial independence and continues to inspire me in her ongoing ability to embrace new challenges. My dad, who taught me to both love books and always question people who claim to know more than you do. My sister, whose bravado I channeled more than once during this process. And the many branches of my extended official and acquired family. While it is somewhat embarrassing, this book took many years to complete— what with all that work getting in the way—and as such I am grateful to the many people along the way who listened to our ideas, plans, and dreams for it; you all know who you are. There were a lot of you over the years, and your willing ears and support contributed to the final product more than you know, so, in addition to all the folks we have jointly thanked, a heartfelt thank-you to Sarah (Sam), Kate, Melanie and Mark, Janelle, Shoni and Nathan, Zoe, Lindsay, Josephine, Dr. Glenda, and the women in my book club. My feline alter ego, Pluto the Wonderkitty, is the best writing companion a girl could hope for, even if he encourages napping over accomplishing.

And of course, my darling Martin, who is willing to put up with both my relentless day-to-day business advice and my overworked self. I hope you know how much I love you. Finally, to the next generation of would-be businesswomen, in particular Pia and Djuna: Maybe someday this will come in handy.

❋ *Lauren thanks:*

First and foremost, Emira, without whom—well, none of this would ever have begun. Thank heavens for the intuition that told me you were not only a fiercely intelligent, gorgeous, and endlessly resourceful friend but that I could trust you with my life and livelihood. There's no one I would rather have shared all of this with. Until that first "Eureka!" moment when we decided to embark on this journey together, I never imagined that business could so capture my heart and soul. Thank you for inspiring me to reach further, every day.

My beloved family, both immediate and extended, who have blessed me with so much. My brother John and sister Margaret, who help me think about things from fresh perspectives, and make me laugh till I cry—I couldn't ask for more inspiring and beautiful siblings. My father, for so many things, but especially your love of words, your courage, and your encouragement. You taught me more than you know about the art and craft of writing. My mother, for teaching me so much about business—from finance and time management to customer service and ethics—without me even catching on that that's what you were up to, and for all the other teachings that could fill another book. My grandparents, especially Grandma MacLeod, whose tough, no-nonsense approach to life helped every one of the MacLeod girls, myself included, grow up knowing we could do anything the boys could (and possibly a few other things besides). A special note of thanks, too, to my aunt Gayle Broad, for her insights and encouragement.

My dear friends, who have given me endless support on this journey—you left me to my writing when I needed solitude, dragged me away from the computer when it was time to call it quits, and perked me up when I was on the verge of being overwhelmed: Day and Nicole; Patty and Justin; Trent; Phoebe, Martin, Amiel, and Miriam; Jenny and Nicole; Jake; Abi and Doug; Frank; Cheryl and Brian. Special thanks to Noah, who held me steady during one of the most challenging projects I've tackled, with characteristic grace, compassion, and good humor. Countless others have offered friendly ears, shoulders, hugs, and nudges along the way; I wish I could thank you all, but the music is starting to play me offstage.

I simply could not have done this without you. I love you all. Thank you from the bottom of my heart.

About the Authors

LAUREN BACON AND EMIRA MEARS co-founded Raised Eyebrow Web Studio in February 2000, and at that time couldn't imagine calling themselves the bosses of anyone. They now lead a team of five, and they have developed a reputation for designing elegant and user-friendly websites for nonprofit organizations and small businesses. Together, they  co-edited Soapboxgirls.com, a monthly e-zine and blog, from 2000 through 2006. They now blog regularly about small business issues at www.laurenandemira.com.

Lauren started her design career during the web's infancy, learning the ropes from a web-designer roommate. Her first website was for the UNBC Women's Centre. Lauren now has a number of high-profile designs gracing the web and has become a sought-after speaker.

Emira has carved herself a niche as a web strategist, offering savvy and creative advice to clients ranging from international online retailers to grassroots non-profits. She is a published freelance writer who has contributed to a range of publications including *Bitch, Venus,* and *Herizons* magazines.

INDEX